With Best Wishes —

Ann Souter Pickering

&

Pollyanna
Pickering

Giant Pandas

永 and 永

Sleeping Dragons

大
熊
猫

The Wolong Panda
Private Collection (UK)

THE WILD PANDA OF FENTENGXIAO

Giant Pandas
 And 永

Sleeping Dragons

大熊猫

Pollyanna Pickering

TEXT BY

Anna-Louise Pickering

FOREWORD BY VIRGINIA McKenna, THE BORN FREE FOUNDATION

PREFACE BY STUART CHAPMAN, CONSERVATION OFFICER, WWF-UK

OTTER HOUSE

For My Gran
Who stayed at home in England and worried

First published in Great Britain in 1996 by
Otter House,
a division of Otter House Limited
Station Yard, Queen Street, Exeter EX4 3TE

Designed by Sue Stainton

British Library Cataloguing in Publication Data
Pickering, Pollyanna
  Giant pandas and sleeping dragons
  1. Pandas - China   2. China - Description and travel
  I. Title II. Pickering, Anna-Louise
  599 . 7 ' 4443 ' 0951

ISBN 0 9529369 0 9

Typeset in Great Britain by Rosemary Lee, Otter House, Exeter, Devon
Colour reproduction by Peninsular Repro Ltd, Exeter, Devon
Printed in Great Britain by Staples Colour Printers, Kettering
Bound in Great Britain by Hartnolls Ltd, Bodmin

FOREWORD

I opened the book and I saw the endearing, enchanting images of Pollyanna's pandas. I began to read Anna-Louise's fascinating, amusing and informed diaries and I knew I was about to travel with them both on an unforgettable and, perhaps, unrepeatable journey, exploring a different culture and a different land.

The impact of this journey was also, for me, an emotional one. Only a few months ago I had been in three major city zoos in China and had seen the panda, the national treasure, the symbol of endangered wildlife, adored and revered by thousands, languishing in dim concrete worlds, shadows behind glass or bars. Many seemingly withdrawn, one seriously disturbed. I had promised myself that, one day, I should see these extraordinary and wonderful creatures in the environment nature had assigned them. I hoped, I prayed, that this could not be the whole story. Now I know that it is not.

In the reserves of Wolong and of Fentengxiao they are fiercely protected by dedicated Chinese people, and in their hospitals and breeding centres the animals receive the best possible care. Of course they lack freedom but this is planned for future offspring.

It seems extraordinary that an animal of such immense and popular appeal could be reduced to the status of an 'endangered species'. If creatures we love suffer that fate, what about the others?

I believe that this book will awaken the sleeping dragon on the mountain top and awaken all of us as well. It is not enough to care about the cuddly panda in the cage. Pollyanna and Anna-Louise have illuminatingly shown us that if we love it as much as we say we do we must allow it to be itself, and live as nature intended.

Virginia McKenna
The Born Free Foundation

*I wouldn't have
known a tragopan
pheasant from a
tufted deer, but I felt
fairly certain that
there would be no
mistaking a panda if
I ever saw one . . .
certainly it never
could be confused
with any other
animal in the world.
The markings are
unmistakable.*

RUTH HARKNESS
THE LADY AND THE PANDA
(1938)

PREFACE

I t is rare to find a book that captures the essence of a place so vividly as *Giant Pandas and Sleeping Dragons*. During the two years I spent at the Wolong nature reserve in China training rangers and guards, I encountered on a daily basis many of the sights, smells and sounds captured in Anna-Louise Pickering's descriptive text and Pollyanna Pickering's evocative illustrations – but I failed to capture on paper the literal translation of my surroundings. As close as one can get to boarding a flight to western China tomorrow, and then travelling to the shrinking habitat of the panda in the most easterly edge of Tibet's plateau, a delve into this book is the next best thing.

My venture into this region was necessitated by a very real and immediate threat to giant pandas in the wild, caused by an unsustainable demand for species which live alongside them in their mountaintop hideaways. Animals such as the taikin, musk deer and Asiatic black bear are valued in traditional Chinese recipes, so their numbers are suffering greatly at the hands of poachers. The irony for the giant panda is that although it is not targeted itself (because it has no traditional use), it falls victim to snares set for the other unfortunate species.

Thanks to the creation of thirteen special reserves – and more are planned – large areas of panda habitat have been protected from over-zealous logging interests. The Chinese government is to implement a conservation plan which seeks to double the number of reserves and create a series of natural corridors that will link isolated panda populations. This has the backing of WWF and is a positive step forward in the conservation of this rare and enigmatic animal. Securing existing and future reserves from the unwanted attentions of poachers is a battle far from won, however, and it remained the most critical issue of all.

Efforts to breed pandas in captivity have resulted in many successes, but the captive population of around one hundred animals is not self-sustaining, and plans to release captive-born pandas into the wild are a long way off. Apart from anything else, they are notoriously difficult to breed in captivity, although there is no evidence to suggest that this is a problem for the wild animal. The future of the giant panda, therefore, lies in conserving it in its natural and rightful place – the wet and windless mountains of western China.

This book will transport you effortlessly to that magnificent area, and I am sure you will be enchanted by every page that you turn.

Stuart Chapman
Conservation Officer, WWF-UK

CONTENTS

PREPARING FOR THE JOURNEY
© BRAMPTON STUDIOS LTD

I N 1992 wildlife artist Pollyanna Pickering travelled to the heart of the Sichuan province of China to study and paint one of the most appealing and elusive of all animals, the giant panda.

This journey was planned as part of an ongoing series of expeditions to study, and record in paintings, endangered species in their natural habitats around the world. Earlier working trips had been made over a six-year period to study the big cats of Africa and India, and polar bears in the frozen wastes of the high Arctic. On each of these journeys I accompanied Pollyanna to document and photograph our travels, as well as to provide moral support.

Organising the journey to China proved harder than we envisaged. We contacted numerous travel companies but could find no-one who could transport us to any of the few last remaining natural reserves of the wild panda, situated on the borders of the Tibetan plateau in Sichuan province. Even the World Wide Fund for Nature, which gives financial support to one of the largest reserves, was unable to provide us with any practical help.

Eventually, after nearly six months of telephone calls and letters, the Chinese Embassy provided us with a contact and we were able to organise flights and hire a driver and an interpreter. It then remained for us to make contact with the two reserves we particularly wished to visit: Wolong, the largest of the government reserves and the most accustomed to welcoming foreign visitors and, in contrast, Fentengxiao, one of the smallest reserves, situated in an area which had only been opened to Western travellers for eight months. In order to obtain the necessary visas, permits and documentation we had to convince the authorities that Pollyanna wished to make a serious study of pandas and that we could be trusted not to damage the fragile environment.

In the spring of 1994 we finally began our journey. Weighed down with luggage that included Pollyanna's sketching equipment, my cameras and notebooks, clothing to see us through temperatures ranging from ninety degrees in the city to below freezing in the mountains, large quantities of toilet rolls and enough medical supplies to equip a small hospital, we flew from Heathrow to Hong Kong to begin our expedition.

The following is an account of our journey through Sichuan province in search of pandas, with extracts from the diaries I kept along the way, a selection of our photographs, and some of the field sketches Pollyanna made during our travels.

The second section of the book shows the end result – the collection of paintings inspired by the wildlife and landscapes of China, completed for a major exhibition staged in the summer of 1995.

Anna-Louise Pickering
Daughter and Business Partner

THE JOURNEY

Chapter One

W大熊猫

E flew out to China in the spring of 1994, breaking our journey for one night in Hong Kong. Our second flight took us from Hong Kong to Chengdu, capital city of Sichuan province.

Fossil records show that giant pandas could once be found throughout China, their range extending into northern Burma, northern Vietnam and Thailand. Now, however, numbers and habitat have dwindled until all the remaining wild pandas can be found in a few isolated pockets – the majority in the mountains on the fringe of the Sichuan basin. Home to over one hundred million people, this province in the southwest of China is slightly larger than France, though it accounts for just one-seventeenth of China's total territory. Chinese leader Deng Xiaoping was born here in 1904 and his home province has been the testing ground for many of his economic reforms. Bordered to the west by Tibet, with the Yunnan province to the south, large areas still remain unexplored by Westerners, with many regions remaining completely out of bounds to foreigners.

Day One

On reaching Hong Kong's Kai Tak airport, we hand over our tickets at what we think is the relevant booking desk. Our flight tickets, issued in the United Kingdom, are in Cathay Pacific folders. The immaculately dressed girl behind the counter greets us with a toothpaste smile and opens the folders. Seconds later she drops them on the counter as if in fear of contamination, her smile frozen at the edges. We are not it seems flying with Cathay Pacific as the folders would indicate, but with a small subsidiary company rejoicing in the unlikely name of Dragonair. Dragonair? She points us in the right direction. We head into the depths of the airport terminal as instructed. We stop, we ask again. Eventually we locate a small desk in the far corner – Dragonair is identified by its logo, an emaciated scarlet dragon which appears to be maintaining an expression of cheerful optimism despite recent electrocution.

We collect our boarding cards and clear passport control and the usual security checks without incident. Half an hour later we flee back to the security check desk at great speed.

永

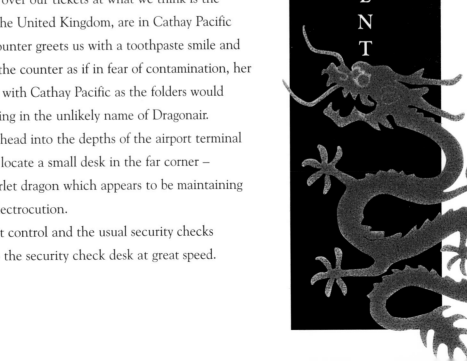

Pollyanna has abandoned her handbag in the X-ray equipment, a fact we only discover while trying to purchase a cup of jasmine tea. In addition to all her money, traveller's cheques and passport, the bag also contains her boarding pass, visas, immunisation certificates, lipstick and more of life's essentials. It is now surrounded by a worried looking group of six airport officials who have not risked opening it. We retrieve the handbag and leave, passport and sanity intact. This bodes well for navigating our way through the wilds of the Chinese countryside with seven pieces of luggage. Although Pollyanna will not complete any original paintings while we are out in China, she is hoping to find plenty of opportunity to make sketches, and is therefore carrying enough art materials to stock a shop. Thick sheaves of tinted sketching paper and crisp hand-finished water-colour papers are filling a bulging portfolio, which will double as a drawing-board. A large canvas satchel holds pencils, pastels and water-soluble crayons, which can be used to create washes of colour at the stroke of a brush. A few other basic requirements jostle for space in my camera bag alongside my cameras – a jar to hold water, sharpeners and bulldog clips. As Pollyanna will not trust her supplies to the hold – we can lose all our clothes and medical supplies in transit but not her precious brushes and paints – the bags are stacked uncomfortably under our seat in the cramped confines of the plane.

A safe if bumpy landing is made in Chengdu at midday. The two-hour flight has passed in a flash; we have been kept thoroughly entertained by the charming English translations in the in-flight magazine provided for our journey.

Chengdu is hot, well over 80°F. We make our way to our overnight hotel. The city is much larger than I had expected. The huge, modern hotel is also something of a surprise. Called the Minshan, and newly built, it is polished and gleaming, both inside and out. The other guests milling in and out of the air-conditioned, marble-floored lobby are mainly American tourists, stopping off *en route* to Tibet. Their bright holiday clothing contrasts sharply with the dark, tailored suits of Hong Kong businessmen, here to take advantage of the newly relaxed Chinese economic policy. Our room is large and luxuriously furnished in tasteful shades of cream and beige; a huge picture window gives a panoramic view across the dusty city. Directly opposite our window brightly coloured hot-air balloons hold long banners of Chinese characters –

we learn later that these are a picturesque equivalent of our advertising hoardings.

We return to the lobby to meet our interpreter who is to travel with us throughout our time in China. We have no idea who to expect and have our fingers crossed that all the arrangements made in England have successfully filtered through to Chengdu. We are also hoping that we will take to the stranger who is to be our travelling companion for the best part of a month. In the event we are met by a friendly and cheerful young woman, wearing a baseball cap and a wide smile. Her name is Wu Xiangjin, but she helpfully suggests that we call her by her adopted English name, Daphne. She takes us outside and introduces our driver, Mr Jing, and the four-wheel drive vehicle that will transport us on our journey. Mr Jing greets us with a solemn politeness. He is smartly dressed in a jacket and tie, his shoes as gleaming as the vehicle he is in charge of. We learn that he does not speak any English. Daphne translates our greetings.

As we are scheduled to drive into the countryside the next day, we make our way to the Baihou Dalou, the largest departmental store in Chengdu, in order to purchase one or two last minute supplies. Driving the length of Remnin Nan Lu, the main boulevard of the city, under the ever watchful eye of the giant statue of Chairman Mao, we reach the store. Impressively fronted by marble lions, with a red carpet leading up the flight of steps to the entrance doors, we are surprised to find that the inside is less Harrods more indoor market. Rows of small stalls and counters sell every conceivable kind of food and drink – from delicate Chinese pastries decorated with brightly coloured icing, to imported Scotch whisky and Russian vodka. We buy some bottled water and two china mugs with matching lids. These come with a thick layer of dust at no extra charge, as it appears does much in the store. The dust is all-pervasive, caused by the poor quality of much of the road surface, coupled with the vast amount of traffic. Our brief shopping trip ends with a visit to the ladies' fashion department, where we discover that the mannequins are tall and pale with blonde hair. Somewhat disconcertingly they bear a stronger resemblance to me than Daphne.

Returning to the car we drive on through Chengdu. Daphne is to take us to a restaurant which has been 'tourist approved' by the company she works for, the Chengdu Overseas Tourism Corporation. The roads are dusty and crowded and the traffic drives on the left. Except when it

BRIGHTLY COLOURED HOT-AIR BALLOONS HOLD LONG BANNERS OF CHINESE CHARACTERS.

DAPHNE, OUR INTERPRETER AND MR JING, OUR DRIVER.

BELOW: THE EVER WATCHFUL EYE OF THE GIANT STATUE OF CHAIRMAN MAO.

BALLCOCKS ON 'PLUMBERS' ROW'.

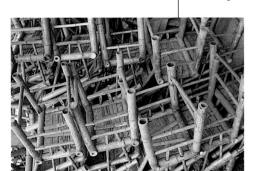

BAMBOO CHAIRS AND TABLES ARE STACKED IN IMPOSSIBLY HIGH PILES, TEETERING AGAINST THE WALLS.

SMALL GROUPS OF MEN INTENT ON THEIR GAMES OF MAH JONG.

doesn't. The cyclists steer in all directions, weaving in and out of lanes of cars, lorries and buses, seemingly impervious to danger. I am enthralled by the narrow streets, the houses, the traffic, the people, the exquisitely painted Chinese characters above the shops. I gaze out of the car windows eager to absorb the atmosphere of my surroundings. The sounds of an unfamiliar language fill the air and a mixture of aromas drifts in through the open window, some new to my senses, others suspiciously familiar. We are held up for a short while in a queue of traffic on a small side street, and I peer eagerly out at the open-fronted shops. Above each store front hangs a row of mysterious gold and silver spheres of varying sizes, suspended from poles. I wonder what mystical Oriental purpose they serve. Do they bring luck? Or are they cooking utensils? Perhaps for use in traditional Chinese medicine? I look deeper into the interiors of the shops, the contents common to all of them are a chaotic mix of lengths of piping, rolls of linoleum, tiles and taps. I look back at the spheres and realise that in fact they are unlikely to protect the shop owners or anybody else from evil spirits. They are ballcocks. We are on 'plumbers' row'.

As we drive through the city, we see many rows of shops supplying the identical product or service grouped together on the same street: hairdressers, electrical goods, tools and seventeen shops in a row all selling safes.

The 'tourist approved' restaurant is in Wangjiang park, set on the edge of the lake above a traditional tea house. Outside, bamboo chairs and tables are stacked in impossibly high piles, teetering against the walls. Small groups of elderly men squat between them, intent on their games of Mah Jong. Inside, the decor is palatially grand. Heavy red velvet curtains hang at the windows behind high-backed, ornately carved mahogany chairs. A party of Japanese tourists are the only other guests. They seem pleased to have our company and, amid much merriment, try out a few English sentences, and buy us bottles of the local beer. When the food starts to arrive we dig in eagerly. It is excellent. Sichuan province is renowned for producing some of the best cuisine in China. Hot spices, garlic and chillies feature in liberal quantities. A vast amount of food is set before us, the dishes as varied as the patterned plates. Highlights include strips of ginger in a mild clear sauce, spicy chicken in honey, mange tout peas in a black bean sauce and a wide selection of local green vegetables. Lowlights include hot cucumber stewed with lumps of pork fat. The whole meal is washed down with a bottle of locally produced Great Wall wine, which the restaurant owner proudly tells us has recently won an export award in Beijing.

That evening we leave the hotel for a twilight constitutional around the city streets. This necessitates dodging the rows of hawkers and street peddlers who have materialised outside the hotel as soon as daylight faded. They boast a bewildering range of goods for sale: real and fake antiques, a selection of herbal medicines and, on every stand, a few copies of Chairman Mao's little red book. There are fortune tellers and street masseurs, all shouting in Chinese, and occasionally in English, though the individual words are lost in the overall cacophony of noise. As far as we can make out the masseurs are threatening 'I kill your back'. We wend our way through the stalls, managing to limit our purchases to one bottle of essential balm which promises a cure for all ills and, unusually, can be swallowed or applied externally. Strolling on we reach a small park. In one corner family groups are gathered round a few small but brightly lit amusement rides for children – dodgem cars, swings and a carousel. A much larger crowd is gathered in the opposite corner of the park and we hurry over to see what is causing all the excitement. It is an American tourist. We provide a brief respite for him merely by existing. We encounter many people on our walk in the park, all friendly and outgoing and very keen to practise their English. Many are extremely fluent, but back outside the Minshan I become engaged in a conversation which seems to concern the cost of hiring a camel in England. It is perhaps just as well that Daphne will be joining us again tomorrow for the start of our journey proper.

A VAST AMOUNT OF FOOD WAS SET BEFORE US.

CHENGDU IS A CITY OF BICYCLES.

CHAIRMAN MAO'S "LITTLE RED BOOK".

Chapter Two

T大熊猫

HE Wolong National Reserve in the Wenchuan district of Sichuan is the largest and most celebrated of the Chinese nature reserves. It nestles in the Qoinglai Mountains, 3,700 metres above sea level. Designated an international biosphere reserve, it is home to two hundred and thirty species of birds, as well as at least thirty-four varieties of reptiles and amphibians, and ninety-six different mammals, including the highly endangered golden monkey and white lipped deer. Largely funded by the World Wide Fund for Nature, Wolong also receives money from other sources, including the Chinese government. Covering an area of two thousand square kilometres of wooded mountains and steep-sided river valleys, the reserve is home to an estimated one hundred and forty giant pandas. It is here that the most detailed studies of pandas have been made by both Chinese and Western scientists, including Dr George Schaller, who has dedicated much of his life to studying the wild pandas of Wolong. It is from the research carried out in this reserve that we gain most of our knowledge of the habits and behaviour of the panda.

A captive breeding programme was initiated in 1983 at the Hetoaping Station at Wolong – also the headquarters of the China Research and Conservation Centre for the Giant Panda. To date five cubs have been successfully reared to adulthood at the breeding station. It is hoped that future captive bred pandas will be successfully released into the wild to supplement the wild population.

Day Two

We leave the hotel at 7.30 am to drive to the Wolong nature reserve. While loading the luggage into the truck, we meet our very first specimen of native Chinese wildlife. A large brown rat is trotting purposefully along the edge of the wide curved marble step at the entrance to the hotel. Its journey is rudely interrupted when it is spotted by the smartly uniformed hotel doorman, who kicks out with unerring precision. The surprised rat describes a perfect arc through the air to land with uncanny accuracy on top of my feet. I am even more surprised than the rat. I scream, the rat screams. Pollyanna and Daphne do not know what is happening, but scream anyway, we all run

EVERYWHERE IS LUSH AND GREEN. THE GENTLE SLOPES OF THE HILLS ARE PLANTED OUT IN A TERRACED PATCHWORK OF SMALL FIELDS.

WE SEE FARMERS PLOUGHING WITH WATER BUFFALO, BAREFOOT AND ANKLE DEEP IN SOFT GREY MUD.

round in circles. The rat is the first to recover its composure and continues on its original journey. We take slightly longer, but eventually set out on the road to Wolong.

We pass through the congested city centre and out into an area which Daphne informs us is the wealthy suburbs of the city, home to the new Chinese millionaires. To the untrained eye this is hard to spot, as most of the buildings seem to be in the earliest stages of construction – or possibly the last stages of demolition. Heading out into the country, the landscape changes rapidly. The tall blocks of single-room flats give way to single-storey farm dwellings set in mile upon mile of agricultural land. Everywhere is lush and green. The gentle slopes of the hills are planted out in a terraced patchwork of small fields, all beautifully tended. The plants stand in neat rows, a measured distance apart and of equal height. There is not a weed in sight, or a stone out of place. Every spare inch of land has been cultivated in odd, seemingly random, shapes. The crops of maize, sweet potatoes and rice have been planted out to the very limit of available space. We see farmers ploughing with water buffalo, barefoot and ankle deep in soft grey mud; men and women sowing, weeding and fertilising the precious crops by hand. The flourishing greenery on each side of the road bears witness to the fact that the lowlands of Sichuan province form the most productive agricultural area of China. The climate is temperate, the soil rich and fertile and capable of supporting three harvests a year. One of the world's oldest irrigation systems carries water from the network of rivers and streams. Back at home, we came across the translation of a verse written by a half-forgotten local Chinese poet:

THE LAND THAT TIME FORGOT
IN THE COLLECTION OF MR & MRS HALIL (UK)

Both rain and drought

follow the will of the people

famine is unknown

Time has never seen a lean year

Everyone knows it as Heaven on earth

Driving through the immaculate and thriving farmland, I could understand why the poet was moved to write such glowing lines in praise of his homeland.

We have only just begun our journey, but already Pollyanna is finding inspiration in every tumble-down farm building and herd of oxen, and above all in the faces of the people we see hard at work tending the crops. Every few miles Mr Jing is compelled to make another emergency stop so that Pollyanna can clip a fresh piece of paper to her board and create an image of the countryside in a few brief strokes. In order to sketch the people candidly and discreetly, Pollyanna does not take out her full range of pencils, pastels and watercolours. Instead, she uses her fountain pen, capturing the character in each face in simple lines, sometimes returning to the sheets later to add detail, or a wash of colour. We find that it is less intrusive for Pollyanna to record the people we meet on paper, than for me to take out my camera and start taking photographs. Every farm and smallholding is a vision of a pastoral existence which we believed had long vanished under the wheels of heavy farm machinery. We pause in the courtyards of small temples, the open air thick with the scent of incense smouldering in giant golden urns; the floors swept clean of debris with a stick broom. Inside one temple building we are delighted to discover an embroidered prayer mat depicting two giant pandas, one of them holding a young cub. We hope this is good omen.

Leaving Chengdu behind, we start to attract more and more attention from the people at the roadside. We stop in one small town to photograph a bridge and within minutes a large group has gathered to watch us. I try out one of the few Chinese phrases I have learnt, '*Ni hao*'. My attempt to say hello is greeted with a few seconds of silence, then with gales of laughter. Following advice from the Chinese Embassy we are both dressed simply in quiet clothes in order to blend in with the local people, but it is becoming blatantly obvious that we could not stand out any more successfully if we had chosen to wear full evening dress complete with diamond tiaras. More people arrive to view us, on bicycles, tricycle taxis and on foot. They are swiftly followed by five military policemen. We have caused a traffic jam on the town's main through road and nothing can pass. We move on, leaving the assembled townspeople still wiping tears of laughter from their eyes.

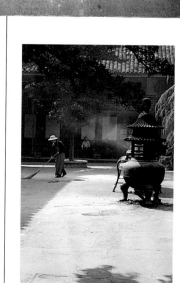

WE PAUSE IN THE COURTYARDS OF SMALL TEMPLES, THE OPEN AIR THICK WITH THE SCENT OF INCENSE SMOULDERING IN GIANT URNS... WE DISCOVER AN EMBROIDERED PRAYER MAT DEPICTING TWO GIANT PANDAS... WE HOPE THIS IS GOOD OMEN.

As we approach Wolong the roads gradually worsen and the landscape becomes more undulating, until finally we see the 'Mountains of the Sleeping Dragon', which form the Wolong reserve, in the distance. According to local legend, a dragon flying over Sichuan many thousands of years ago was so entranced by the local landscape that he chose to lie down and rest there for a while in the midst of the beauty. He fell into a deep sleep and remains there to this day.

Approaching the mountains, Pollyanna can see clearly the inspiration behind the simple figurative work which is typical of the Chinese art she admires so much. Broad strokes of grey and black are used to represent the forms of the mountains, the ragged clouds which cling to their slopes, the lakes and the rivers which course through the deep valleys. This harmonious style of painting, which is still popular today, was largely developed in the Sung Dynasty (970 - 1279). Guo Xi, one of the most successful artists working during this period, believed that the task of the landscape artist was to bring the tranquillity of nature into every home. Pollyanna is hoping that, by the end of her journey, she will be able to follow his advice, written so many centuries before our travels.

It is already turning dark when, after nine hours on the road, we reach the barrier at the entrance to the nature reserve. Our papers are in order and we are allowed through. A tunnel hewn through the mountainside leads us into the reserve. On leaving the tunnel, the pot-holed track turns into a smooth concrete road and we drive for a further hour in relative comfort, until we reach the breeding station. Ahead of us the mountains are charcoal grey shapes, the peaks rising from motionless clouds of white mist. The lights of the breeding station glow softly in the distance and we can just make out a semicircle of white buildings – the pens housing the pandas in the breeding programme. By the time we arrive the light has gone and we are too late to go down and see the pandas. We are met by the director of the reserve and introduced to several of his co-workers, some of whom speak a little English. There are no other visitors staying at the reserve, but we are introduced briefly to Susan, an American naturalist, who has been working at Wolong for a year.

Our driver, Mr Jing, is very familiar with the reserve, having driven vehicles for the BBC during the filming of a recent wildlife documentary in Wolong. He is known to the workers here as 'Jingo', and within seconds of arriving he has joined in an ongoing and riotous card game.

Some food is prepared for us in a small kitchen. Mr Jing rejoins us, and the four of us eat round a rickety wooden table in the adjoining room. Some strips of a thin pasta-like food are hanging above the cooking area in the kitchen window, presumably to dry out for storage. Keen to record everything, I go nearer to take a photograph of the way this dish is being prepared. However, on closer investigation it emerges that the pale strips are not food – they are all that remains of the kitchen curtains.

After the meal we are escorted to our room. The breeding station is relatively well equipped to receive visitors and, though simple, the room is quite adequate. Two single beds stand on a concrete floor. We have electricity and a small private bathroom. We are shown the shower, a metal tank at the top of the tiled wall, with a shower head attached. The workers fill the tank with buckets and show us how to heat the water by plugging the tank into the mains. A length of frayed wire leads directly from the bottom of the tank; the plug on the end is inserted into a socket on the shower wall and the wiring is clearly visible behind the plate. To plug it in while standing on the wet tiles of the shower floor would seem to be risking death by electrocution, or at best a tight perm.

It is now very cold and we are supplied with a small open electric heater. We revel in the heat it provides for a hour or so, but then it expires in a spectacular flash of light. I decide that this would be a good time to retire to bed and venture into the bathroom to brave the shower. Against the odds, I survive. I then spot that the toilet cistern has not refilled after its earlier use (this is easy to ascertain as it does not possess a lid). I wonder if I should have invested in my own ballcock and plumbing supplies when I had the chance in Chengdu but, on standing back, I realise that there is a very simple explanation. It has not refilled because is it not plumbed in. It simply empties through a hole in the wall. While working out how long it will take to refill the tank using my china cup, scooping water across from the sink (the only piece of equipment in the room attached to a water supply), I spot a length of rubber hose attached to the wall. A little mental agility results in our realising that it is in fact not long enough to stretch from the tap of the sink to the toilet cistern, thus speeding the process up considerably.

THE LIGHTS OF THE BREEDING STATION GLOW SOFTLY IN THE DISTANCE.

Chapter Three

T大熊猫

T HE object of Pollyanna's quest, for which we are prepared to brave the hazards of Chinese plumbing, is, of course, the giant panda. Unique to China, and unique within the animal kingdom, the panda's distinctive markings are instantly recognised the world over. Dense creamy white fur covers the body and a broad black band stretches across the shoulders and down the forelegs. The back legs, nose and ears are also black, while small dark eyes peer out inquisitively from coal black patches, giving the panda an appealing look of wide-eyed innocence. Soft and rounded, with a pigeon-toed walk, pandas resemble a child's teddy bear come to life. An adult panda, however, can weigh up to 135 kilograms, measure almost two metres from nose to tail and stand around a metre tall at the shoulder. Naturalists have yet to provide a convincing theory to explain the evolutionary benefit of the panda's improbable markings. These markings do not appear to provide any camouflage in the bamboo forests, even in the black shadows of night. Neither has any definite conclusion been reached on the ancestry of the giant panda. Regarded as a living fossil, it may have evolutionary links to bears or racoons, or stand alone as a separate species. There are thought to be only one thousand pandas left in existence, including the eighty or so in captivity in China and around the world. The Chinese government has now declared the panda a national treasure. It is known internationally as a powerful symbol of the struggle for conservation.

Local legends provide a romantic, if sad, explanation for the panda's distinctive colouring. The story is still told of a time long ago, when all the pandas in China were pure white. A young, beautiful shepherdess lived in Wolong. Good and kind, she was loved by people and animals alike. Often, when she tended to her flock of sheep in the hills, a young panda would come and sit with her. One tragic day a leopard attacked the panda, as it walked with the flock. With no care for her own safety, the young girl fought the leopard, saving the panda, but losing her life in the process. When the other pandas in the forest heard of her death they were distraught. Attending her funeral, they observed the local custom of covering their arms and legs in ashes as a sign of mourning. Weeping at the

永

THREE PANDAS PERCHED ON TOP OF THE WORLD.

graveside, they touched their eyes to wipe away the tears and covered their ears with their paws to block out the sounds of their grief. Wherever they touched themselves with their ash-covered paws, their fur was stained black. It is said that all pandas carry these marks to this day as a mark of respect for the brave young shepherdess.

Day Three

Awake refreshed, having slept well despite the cold. We add several more layers of clothing and make our way down for breakfast. Our first experience of the traditional first meal of the day for the local Chinese population: a cauldron of warm boiled rice, still in the cooking water, which we half drink half slurp out of small pot bowls; steamed bread rolls called *mantou*, slightly reminiscent of white bread rolls back home but denser and less cooked; very highly spiced cold pickled beans and spring onions and a bowl of peanuts. It is 7.00 am and I am craving toast and coffee but, resolutely, I practise my chopstick technique on the peanuts.

After breakfast the workers lead us down to the breeding centre. A statue of three pandas perched on top of the world stands outside the impressive entrance gates. As we pass into the breeding centre we walk over rush mats soaked in disinfectant – a precaution to prevent the transmission of diseases to the rare inhabitants.

The centre consists of a semicircle of pens, each with an indoor and outdoor area, and each housing a panda. Solitary creatures by nature, they are kept separately. There are seventeen in all. After all the months of planning, reading, researching and hoping, it is incredible finally to find ourselves face to face with these rare creatures in the heart of their homeland.

In the first pen is an adult female named Jia Jia. She is sitting placidly in the corner of the open yard and, as we approach, turns her head slowly to look at the newcomers. For a few moments we pause, fact to face, just a few feet away from one another; her small glossy black eyes fixed intently on my face until she turns away again to munch, unconcerned, on a stem of bamboo.

All the enclosures appear clean and well kept but, looking at the vast mountains rising behind the breeding station, we could not help feeling a certain sympathy for Jia Jia and the other pandas chosen for the breeding project. Hopefully, if future breeding programmes prove successful, they will one day contribute towards the survival of their species.

We are introduced to all the other pandas in the centre, including Jia Lin, Jia Jia's first baby, born in 1992, when Jia Jia was fifteen years old. Despite coming relatively late to motherhood (female pandas usually produce their first cub by the age of six) she proved to be an excellent mother, and Jia Lin is now a thriving young adult.

There is a good fifteen-centimetre gap between the bars of each enclosure and Jia Lin can easily reach through with her broad paws. We stroke the fur gingerly, taking great care to avoid the long curving claws – five on each paw. Pollyanna is given permission to sketch freely and we spend hours in front of the pens, concentrating largely on a three-year-old male panda. He is a natural exhibitionist, posing in a variety of positions to attract and hold our attention. We learn that because of our friendship with Mr Jing we have been given special privileges. Wolong has a policy of charging all visitors to the centre to take photographs in order to raise funds for their research work. We are to be treated as honorary Chinese, so I am allowed to take as many photographs as I wish for my fee, instead of being restricted to ten, the normal policy for Westerners. We are extremely grateful for this kindness.

Having spent the whole day sitting in front of the pandas, Pollyanna has already filled a whole sketch pad with detailed line drawings, quick studies and water-colour sketches as well as copious notes on the markings and behaviour of the individual pandas. These sketches will form the references for the exhibition of original paintings which she hopes to complete on her return to the studio. As many of her paintings are quite large – over a metre and a half square – it is impractical to bring the necessary paper and boards for her to work *in situ*. The finished paintings will contain a great deal of detail – not just in the fur of the pandas, but in the surrounding habitat – each frond of fern, each blade of bamboo will be individually and painstakingly painted with tiny brushes. The larger and more complex works will take up to three weeks of solid studio time to finish – time we cannot spare during our stay in China.

. . . Jia Lin can easily reach through with her broad paws. We stroke the fur gingerly, taking great care to avoid the long curving claws – five on each paw.

Pollyanna is packing away her pencils and completed sketches, and we are preparing to walk back up to our room, when we are summoned by the director of the breeding centre. A very special honour is about to be bestowed upon us. We are taken into an enclosed room in a private section of the centre; here we peer through a small window at the top of a wooden door. We can

hardly believe our eyes. In the room beyond is four-month-old panda, the newest arrival at the breeding station. He can barely walk, but is swaying on his still unsteady legs. The little panda is assigned to two keepers and they monitor him twenty-four hours a day. His mother, Dong Dong, gave birth to twins in 1992 and a single cub in 1993, making her the most successful female panda in the history of the centre's captive breeding programme. We are told that her baby has not been shown to any other visitors – not all of the workers at the centre have yet been allowed to see him. We are not allowed to take any photographs, or to stay long enough for Pollyanna to complete any sketches (to her intense frustration) but we feel honoured to have been shown this precious baby, the pride of the breeding centre.

After our evening meal, Pollyanna and I stroll down to the banks of the Pitao river, which flows through the reserve. The landscape has an ethereal beauty in the dusk, with patches of mist hanging motionless on the mountainsides. These appear in the evening light to be without substance, two-dimensional tissue paper shapes in varying shades of soft grey. Pollyanna is still carrying her sketch books, and uses her water-colour pencils to create gentle washes of colour, committing the beauty of the mountains to paper with a few strokes of her brush. Completely surrounded by mountains, the whole area has its weather extremely well organised. The natural

BAMBOO CURTAIN

basin in the centre is practically free of wind. Sichuan is also famed for its night rains, immortalised by local poets throughout the centuries. Dry during the day, a light drizzle begins at dusk. Then the rain falls heavily during the night, stopping again at first light. Down by the water's edge we see several birds: red-tailed chats, white-throated dippers and smaller versions of the magpie with which we are so familiar in England. The magpie was originally brought over from China to England during the last century. We catch a brief glimpse of a skinny chocolate-brown rock squirrel on the opposite side of the river as it disappears over a low wall. Feeling at peace with the world, we scramble back up the river bank and make our way back to our quarters.

The feeling of contentment is not to last. A few moments after our return we see what appears to be a pointed bloated slug writhing on the concrete floor of our room. We remove it – or at least Pollyanna removes it, and I bravely hold the door open. A few more moments pass while we shudder delicately. Pollyanna notices some blood seeping through her sock. She removes her boot to reveal a neat round puncture hole on her ankle which is bleeding copiously. The pointed slug was in fact a giant land leech which had hitched a ride into our room on Pollyanna's leg. She has been leeched. Blood-sucked! Leech saliva contains a natural anaesthetic, as well as anticoagulant, so she had not felt a thing. My well-stocked first-aid kit is locked in the truck. I go in search of Mr Jing who has the keys, but cannot find him, or Daphne, or anyone who speaks sufficient English to tell me his whereabouts. Eventually, I track him down in the middle of another card game and, after much flapping and waving, recover my supplies. I am carrying so much medical equipment – sterilised IV tubing, syringes, surgical gloves, emergency brain surgery kit – that it takes me nearly ten minutes to locate a simple plaster and a tube of antiseptic cream. Meanwhile, Pollyanna continues to lose her life's blood – the anticoagulant in leech saliva is clearly very effective. It is possible to be too close to some kinds of wildlife.

THE LANDSCAPE HAS AN ETHEREAL BEAUTY IN THE DUSK, WITH PATCHES OF MIST HANGING MOTIONLESS ON THE MOUNTAINSIDES.

THE POINTED SLUG WAS IN FACT A GIANT LAND LEECH WHICH HAD HITCHED A RIDE INTO OUR ROOM ON POLLYANNA'S LEG

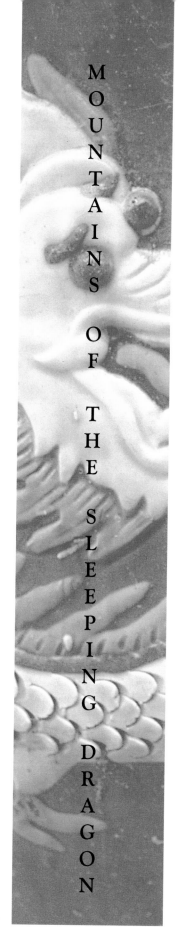

VIEWED from a distance, the mountains of the Wolong reserve look like the ridged back and tail of a gigantic dragon lying across the landscape. It is this, rather than the fact that the mountains house the last remaining specimens of a mythical species, which has earned them the romantic sobriquet 'Mountains of the Sleeping Dragon'.

Dragons, a symbol of luck and life, are a familiar image from Chinese art throughout the ages. The historical existence of a real dragon has never been scientifically accepted, though some have suggested the legends may have grown from sightings of giant lizards, such as the komodo dragon. As we travelled through China, we noticed that the dragon was a frequently used symbol, depicted on carvings and paintings, alongside tigers and bears.

In Imperial China, the dragon was a symbol of the power of the emperor. Dragons are largely viewed in China as benign symbols of luck and good fortune, despite their terrifying appearance. In legend dragons are empowered with the ability to change form at will, and to influence the weather. Seen as intermediaries between the earth and sky, they live in springs, rivers, seas and clouds. If a dragon is insulted or angered by human actions, it will retire from the earth and hide in the waters to hibernate, thus causing a drought. To awaken the sleeping dragon, and bring forth the rains needed to grow the crops, it is necessary to make a great noise. This belief has given rise to the traditional Chinese New Year celebrations, in which a huge mock dragon is paraded down the streets, to the accompaniment of loud music and the banging of drums.

They are often seen on everyday items such as cooking utensils and plant pots. The dragon is one of the creatures of the cycle of years in the Chinese calendar which are all named for animals, the full list being: rat, ox, tiger, rabbit, dragon, snake, horse, ram, monkey, rooster, dog and pig. It is curious that just one mythical creature is included in an otherwise down to earth group.

The Zoozhua, a commentary on spring and autumn animals written by Zuo Ouimings around 600 BC, records the keeping of dragons and notes that, between 2600 and 2200 BC, monarchs employed specialists to keep and breed dragons at court. Many Chinese pharmacies still claim to sell fossilised dragons' teeth.

Interestingly, many Western scientists believed until the mid-nineteenth

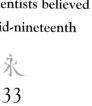

33

century that the panda (extremely rare even then) was a mythical animal from Chinese legend. They initially dismissed the reports of a living black and white bear which started to filter out of China towards the end of the century. With these thoughts in my mind, I would have not been too surprised to see the scaly form of a dragon rising from the mists clinging to the slopes of the mountains . . .

Day Four

Over the next few days we are to make our first forays into the natural habitat of the wild panda. It is very important for Pollyanna to experience and study the natural habitat of her subjects before painting them. Seeing the bamboo groves, where the pandas feed, and the springs and streams where they stop to drink, will give her a picture of their lifestyle and environment which cannot be gained from reading books. The plants and trees which grow in their habitat will provide Pollyanna with the backgrounds and settings in which she will place her animal subjects. This means climbing from the breeding station to the higher regions of the mountainside, where the bamboo grows in abundance. Our dream is to see a wild panda, but with approximately seventy pandas in two thousand square kilometres, the odds are not good.

A special breakfast is prepared to give us strength for our first trek: wok-fried omelettes with chopped spring onions and prawn crackers; along with the customary rice, bread and peanuts. During this meal, one of the workers at Wolong describes to Daphne the route we must take. None of them can be spared from the centre, so the four of us will have to make our way alone. A list of instructions follows:

> *We are to climb to an altitude of three thousand metres*
> *We must take provisions*
> *We must take a torch, as it may be dark in the holes*

Holes?
I ask through Daphne, are the holes very small?
No, but the water in them may be very deep this time of year.
Water?

With some trepidation we load our backpacks with food, water, flashlights, cameras and sketch pads, and thus weighed down set out for the mountain. Mr Jing has spent three years in the

Chinese army, so for him this should be no more than a gentle afternoon stroll.

We drive forty kilometres along the track to the base of the slope we are to climb and leave the vehicle by a small bridge. Crossing the river on foot, we set off up a narrow track, fairly steep and rough with scree. We are already quite high and at this altitude the air is noticeably thin. We quickly become breathless and find ourselves making frequent rest stops. We soon climb out of the evergreen forests which cover the lower slopes where tangles of silver lichens drip from the overhanging branches, and emerge into the broad-leafed woodland and bamboo groves of the higher slopes. Pollyanna goes into artistic raptures over the many colourful mosses and lichens and takes advantage of the breaks to begin sketching the trees and plants. It is spring so the mountains are full of flowers. We pass rhododendron bushes bending under the weight of the blooms, and peer closely at smaller delicate orchids. Many of the wild plants are familiar to us, such as wild strawberry plants and ferns. Thickets of bamboo grow alongside the path we are following.

The 'holes', which have been giving me nightmares ever since breakfast, turn out to be tunnels hacked through the mountainside. They are dark and narrow, but high enough to stand upright for most of the time. Some are very long, so the torches are essential. The water we were warned about is a small stream of melting snow running down from the peaks of the mountains. It is ankle deep along most of the path, occasionally reaching mid-calf, though not deep enough to cause us any serious discomfort.

The higher we progress, the steeper and rougher the track becomes. In some places we have to clamber over rock falls and find tenuous foot holds on tree roots and in rock crevices when the path disappears completely. We make steady but slow progress for around three hours, moving in procession: Pollyanna and Daphne leading the way, then me, with Mr Jing bringing up the rear, labouring under the weight of the bulk of the provisions.

Suddenly, we are overtaken. An elderly man is hurrying up the path, carrying a huge basket on his back. Panting for breath, we pull in to the side to allow him to pass. Daphne chats to him briefly and we learn that he lives halfway up the mountainside and walks down to the small settlement at the base each day to buy food. Looking doubtfully at us out of the corner of his eye, he offers to make us all a cup of tea, when (or if) we reach his home. He guesses that we should reach him in around an hour. Given that I can hardly breathe, my own estimate is slightly less optimistic. He disappears along the path and, spurred on by the thought of refreshment, we follow

WILD FLOWERS OF CHINA
IN THE COLLECTION OF MR G M BIGGIN (UK)

WE PASS RHODODENDRON BUSHES
BENDING UNDER THE WEIGHT OF THE
BLOOMS, AND PEER CLOSELY AT
SMALLER DELICATE ORCHIDS . . .
THICKETS OF BAMBOO GROW
ALONGSIDE THE PATH WE ARE
FOLLOWING.

DRINKING PHIALS OF HONEY AND GINSENG TO GIVE US ENERGY.

TO OUR SURPRISE AND DELIGHT HE ALSO OFFERS TO PREPARE US A MEAL.

A HUGE BLACK POT OF HOME-MADE NOODLES, FRESHLY COOKED OVER A FIRE, IS BROUGHT OUT OF THE FARMHOUSE.

him, albeit at a considerably slower pace.

Finally, we claw our way up to a small wooden farmhouse, set on a slight plateau on the mountainside. Our new acquaintance appears in the doorway and invites us to sit down at a wooden table outside. True to his promise, he brings out huge flasks of boiling water and makes us each a bowl of tea with freshly picked green leaves. We are more than grateful.

To our surprise and delight he also offers to prepare us a meal. A huge black pot of home-made noodles, freshly cooked over a fire, is brought out of the farmhouse. He mixes them with a small amount of burning red chilli paste and a dash of soy sauce. Added to this are strips of tender bacon and sliced green beans cooked in honey. The food is delicious, we are all ravenous after the climb. More tea is served, made from the fresh spring water which flows from a rocky outcrop behind the farm.

I regain my breath and start to study our surroundings. Outside the wooden farmhouse rows of chillies and beans are hung to dry in the crisp air, to be preserved for future use. Faded black lettering covers the timber. A few thin white chickens peck idly at the sparse frozen ground. I come to the conclusion that this must be one of the cleanest places left on planet earth. Remote and inaccessible, we are miles from any heavy industry. Being within the boundaries of the Wolong reserve, it also seems likely that it will remain undisturbed for years to come. I expect to live for an additional ten years simply for having breathed the air.

Pollyanna breathes a lot of the air. She becomes euphoric. This is Heaven on Earth. Paradise. She wants to leave the rat race and stay here for ever, living on the land, drinking the spring water, breathing in the air. I am less sure. Beautiful and clean, it is also only eight degrees centigrade just after midday in spring. In winter it must appear a far less hospitable place to set up home, though, under a blanket of snow, the mountainsides must seem even more beautiful and ethereal.

Well rested and refuelled, we say our farewells and continue our slow progress up the mountain until we reach the still-frozen blocks of snow which remain near the summit. The views across the mountains are spectacular and my camera works overtime trying to capture the landscape which stretches away from us. However, aside from an occasional glimpse of a bird – wrens, wagtails and a lone monal pheasant which scurries out of our

THIS IS HEAVEN ON EARTH.
PARADISE. DRINKING THE SPRING
WATER, BREATHING IN THE AIR.

path – we have not seen any wildlife. Not a whisker of a panda has come our way, even in the 'feeding grounds' of bamboo we have passed through. I am illogically disappointed. Despite having the odds stacked against us, I had harboured secret hopes of finding traces at least – perhaps fresh droppings or chewed stems of bamboo.

We make our way precariously back down the mountainside. The climb down is far quicker, despite the loose scree that makes the going very slippery in places. We are back at the base in less than half the time it took to reach the summit. We return to the truck and head back to the breeding station to visit the pandas and plan our schedule for exploring more areas of mountainside over the next few days.

TRUE TO HIS PROMISE, HE BRINGS
OUT HUGE FLASKS OF BOILING WATER
AND MAKES US EACH A BOWL OF TEA
WITH FRESHLY PICKED GREEN LEAVES.

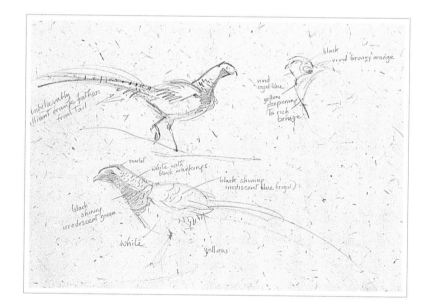

Chapter Five

O大熊猫

OUR remaining few days at Wolong are spent studying the pandas in the breeding centre and making a series of treks into the mountains to look, unsuccessfully, for any traces of the wild giant pandas.

On our last day at Wolong we are making our way back down the mountain slopes towards the reserve when we catch the briefest glimpse of ginger fur vanishing into the undergrowth. We have spotted a panda at last – though not the familiar black and white animal we had hoped to find. We stay in the area for over an hour watching for any further movement, but we see no further sign of the animal which we are sure was a red panda.

The red panda is probably the closest living relative of the giant panda. Like its larger cousin it is endangered, and the Chinese government has officially accorded full protection to the species although its exact status is not known. Despite being an extremely attractive animal it receives comparatively little world attention.

The red panda was known to Western zoologists long before the giant panda was discovered. The first foreigner to see one in the wild was probably Nathaniel Wallich, a Danish botanist, who sent a skin back to Europe in 1821. It is from the red panda that both animals took their name – though the origin of the word is mysterious. The local name is more usually given as *wah*, an approximation of their call.

In common with the giant panda, bamboo forms the staple diet of the red panda, contributing eighty to ninety-five per cent of all they consume. They are more choosy however, concentrating only on the tender leaves, nipping off one or two at a time and chewing each one thoroughly, ignoring the less nutritious woody stems. Largely nocturnal, they will also eat grasses, berries, especially the fruit of the wild cherry, roots and grubs. There are some reports of them hunting for small birds. Like cats, red pandas move almost silently. They have a thick, banded tail, pointed ears and a masked face, closely resembling a racoon. The bushy tail, which is almost as long as the body, often serves the red panda as a cushion on which it can rest its chin when settling down to sleep. In cold weather the tail is used to cover the panda's nose like a blanket. Around the size of a fox, an adult red panda

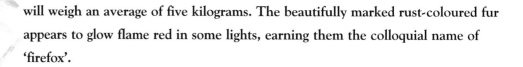

will weigh an average of five kilograms. The beautifully marked rust-coloured fur appears to glow flame red in some lights, earning them the colloquial name of 'firefox'.

Day Six

Returning from the mountains in the late afternoon, we tell the workers at the breeding centre of our great excitement at having very briefly spotted a red panda. The staff express surprise at our interest in red pandas. Does Pollyanna also intend to paint them? Yes? Well, would we like to see some?

We are led out of the giant panda breeding station, across the river, and up a long flight of concrete steps. We pass through two doors and find ourselves in a large walled paddock some eight hundred metres square. This, we are informed, is the red panda breeding enclosure, built in 1993 for the purpose of comparing the behaviour and reproductive habits of the red and giant pandas. Until that moment we had no idea that Wolong, famous for its attempts to breed the giant panda, was also running a breeding and release programme for red pandas. So much attention is focused on the plight of the giant panda that most visitors to the reserve never express any interest in their smaller relative.

We look eagerly around the paddock, but cannot see a single panda. Our guide smiles and tells us to wait until feeding time. There is, we are told, just a chance that we may be able to spot one or two when the food is put down. Within ten minutes the food has arrived – chunks of bread and a large kettle of milk, which is poured into long plastic drinking troughs. The effect of the food being placed on the ground is immediate and breathtaking. Red pandas come streaming towards us, materialising from holes in the ground, from behind rocks, and swarming down from the branches of the trees. Within half a minute there are fifteen at our feet pushing for space at the troughs, making soft mewling cries. This call, eerily child-like, gave rise to another ancient Chinese name for the red pandas, 'Children of the Mountain'.

When all the bread and milk has been consumed they slowly disperse. Instead of vanishing back into the cover of their dens they sit on the rocks, licking their paws and grooming each

THE EFFECT OF THE FOOD BEING PLACED ON THE GROUND IS IMMEDIATE AND BREATHTAKING.

other. As they are relatively used to people I am able to approach within a few feet to take photographs and Pollyanna is able to sketch to her heart's content. She uses her pastels to capture the vivid colour of their fur as it glows in the evening sunlight.

Several pandas climb with a cat-like grace and agility into the top branches of the trees and settle themselves into a fork to rest, lying still while absorbing the last rays of the evening sun. Recent research, reported by the British couple Keith and Liz Laidler, who have made several documentaries for the BBC while based at Wolong, suggests that red pandas may sunbathe as a way of supplementing the energy from their nutritionally inadequate bamboo diet. The warmth they absorb helps keep their body temperature at the correct level, so reducing the amount of energy needed to survive. Indeed, the red pandas would appear to be so dependent on sunlight as a source of energy that they will only live on the sunny side of the mountains in their range, leaving cold north-facing slopes uninhabited, despite a good food supply.

We are told that the red pandas are left to breed naturally within the enclosure, and that so far the programme has been quite successful. Here, as in the wild, female red pandas make a nest den in a small cave or a hollow tree. Several days before the young are born they carry in grasses and leaves to use as bedding; the pandas continue with this nesting until the young emerge. At birth the cubs weigh 120 grams, slightly more than the young of the giant panda, an animal over twenty times larger! They grow and mature at a much faster rate than their larger cousins, resembling miniature adults at two months old. By three months they can climb trees and are eating bamboo and other solid foods. Four babies have been bred at Wolong and we are lucky enough to see one of the youngsters; it is almost as big as the adults, but still with a soft round face. One of the adult females is also believed to be pregnant again.

We stay watching the pandas until they all retire back into their dens. The light is starting to fade and the drizzle which heralds the night rains is softly falling. We make our way back to our room for what will be our last night at Wolong.

THEIR CALL, EERILY CHILD-LIKE, GAVE RISE TO ANOTHER ANCIENT CHINESE NAME FOR THE RED PANDAS, 'CHILDREN OF THE MOUNTAIN'.

Chapter Six

大熊猫

I T is notoriously difficult for giant pandas to breed successfully in captivity. Aside from any other considerations, it can be very difficult to determine accurately the sex of adult pandas. In 1938 the earliest attempt to breed from pandas in captivity failed, simply because both of the 'pair' of pandas in the Brook Field Zoo in Chicago turned out to be female. This vital piece of information was discovered only during an autopsy following the death of the 'male'.

Female pandas come into season irregularly, usually between mid March and the end of May, and only then for a very brief time. Sometimes they are receptive to the male for as little as forty-eight hours in a year. Occasionally they may come into season a second time later in the year. The subtle changes in behaviour which signal that a female may be ready to mate can easily be missed or misinterpreted. Solitary animals by nature, the pandas are normally kept apart until it is clear that the female is ready to mate. If the keepers fail to recognise the signs there may be no possibility of breeding for a further twelve months.

Various attempts at artificial insemination have been made in some zoos. This method has met with some limited success, but the problems of judging the time when the female is most receptive to fertilisation remain.

Attempts to breed pandas in captivity began in 1955, but it was not until 1963 that the first cub was born in Beijing Zoo. Since then fewer than half of the pandas born in captivity have been reared to adulthood. Outside China, breeding programmes have been even less successful, with Mexico Zoo the only institution to have achieved repeated success in breeding and rearing pandas.

When the breeding station at Wolong was established in the early 1980s it was hoped that by concentrating all the attention and funding on one species, better results could be achieved than had previously been attained in the zoos. The first young panda was bred at Wolong in 1986; we already had a privileged glimpse of the most recent success story – the four-month-old baby we had been shown on day one of our visit.

PERHAPS A BUNCH OF FLOWERS
WOULD HAVE HELPED.

Day Seven

We are due to return to the city of Chengdu for one day of rest before we depart on the next stage of our journey to the natural reserve of Fentengxiao.

We wake early and pack before joining Daphne and Mr Jing for breakfast. Arriving in the dining-room we find everyone in a state of great excitement. The workers have decided that one of the females in the centre is at the peak of her season and is to be 'introduced' to one of the males that morning. Would we like to go down to the pens to witness the 'Mating Ceremony'?

We hurry down to the breeding centre to find that all of the workers, officials and naturalists are gathered around the female's pen. The atmosphere of anticipation is intense. It is quite an honour to be invited to watch the pair of pandas 'making their sexual life', an event hardly ever seen in the wild, and only rarely witnessed in captivity.

The female has been scent marking the trees in her pen and calling to the male in the adjoining enclosure. Her behaviour has been closely monitored over the past few days; this morning she is judged 'ready'. Two workers arrive with ladders and climb up on top of the high walls around the outside enclosure. They are carrying long bamboo poles which they will use to separate the two pandas if all does not go according to plan and one of the pair attacks the other.

The female panda seems restless. She paces up and down, pausing occasionally to sniff at the wall of the pen. One of the workers taps her gently on the back with the end of the bamboo pole. She reacts by crouching down and raising her tail. A murmur of excitement passes through the audience. She is ready.

The male panda has already been brought into the inside pen at the rear of the female's enclosure. We are told that he is to be 'excited' in readiness for the task ahead of him. This is achieved by giving him leaves and bark which have been scented by the female. This will alert him to the fact that there is a receptive female panda nearby.

The great moment arrives. The door at the back of the pen is opened. An expectant hush falls over the assembled crowd. We do not have to wait long. In fact we do not have to wait at all. For all the build up there is very little ceremony to the mating. The male rushes out with unseemly haste and immediately mounts the female. I had been expecting them to greet one another, circle round, maybe nuzzle affectionately. Possibly the female had also been expecting

this for, a mere thirty seconds later, she decides that enough is enough and turns round and cuffs the male round the ear. He backs off and then advances again making a second attempt to mount her. The audience has been holding its breath – I half expect everyone to break into spontaneous applause as he succeeds again. However, the female is still not impressed and turns on him with considerably more aggression. Fearing a fight, the workers use the poles to guide the male back out of the enclosure. Perhaps a bunch of flowers would have helped.

As the door closes behind him, everyone in the centre is congratulating each other; there is much hand shaking and back slapping. It appears that even this brief mating may well be sufficient for the female to have conceived.

The gestation period for pandas is quite brief, around one hundred and forty days, and the females show few outward signs of pregnancy; they may nest build or slightly change their eating habits. All that can be done at Wolong now is to watch and wait. We learn that the gestation period can vary considerably. Female pandas have been known to give birth anywhere between ninety-six and one hundred and sixty eight days after mating. This wide discrepancy would seem to suggest a delayed implantation of the embryo, as seen in some other species. However, naturalists are unsure why this would be an advantage to the panda as they do not rely on a seasonal supply of food.

This morning at Wolong such questions are put aside. There is a tangible sense of elation at the completion of a successful mating ceremony. This mood of celebration is infectious and we leave Wolong in high spirits to begin the drive back to Chengdu.

The long journey back passes remarkably quickly; the first few hours spent in animated discussion of the events at Wolong, with Daphne spiritedly translating everything for Mr Jing. I am put to shame, my knowledge of Chinese so far does not extend much beyond hello (*ni hao*), thank you, (*chia chia*) and a local name for the giant panda, (*shung-wah*). Without Daphne to help, I suspect that this would not get me far.

Mr Jing tells us via Daphne of his attempts to learn English at school. He remembers only a few phrases, including 'thank you very much'. He tells us that the children in Chinese schools are taught a few simple sentences like this by learning a string of Chinese words which have roughly the same sound as the English sentence when spoken aloud. Thus to make the sounds for 'thank

DELICATE JASMINE TEA SERVED FROM GOLDEN URNS.

you very much', the children say in Chinese 'three pills for your mother'. Similarly the phrase 'don't break my heart' has the same sound as 'frostbite is not good for you' in Mandarin.

I realise that by reversing this principle I can add two Chinese phrases to my limited vocabulary. All I need now is to meet a Chinese person whose mother has a headache and is thinking of taking a holiday in the high Arctic.

Our return journey is broken by a couple of stops for petrol. The truck appears to have a bottomless tank. We are carrying a can of fuel in case of emergencies, but never make use of it. The attendants at the petrol stations in the small towns peer in at us with undisguised curiosity. On more than one occasion they insist that we get out and take photographs.

On reaching the city we make a slight diversion to stand in line at the municipal car wash. It is apparently the policy of the local government for all cars returning to the city to be cleaned – in part to keep down the levels of dust. There are a dozen queues of vehicles waiting to be washed with high pressure hoses. Pollyanna leaps out to take a photograph and immediately gets drenched, as does Mr Jing, who has got out to point out any small specks which have been missed. Luckily it is hot in the city, at around 80° F. Having left the bitter cold of Wolong I am still wearing thermal leggings and am very tempted to join them under the spray.

Another persuasive reason for taking an impromptu shower is the fact that I am thick with dust and scruffy and bedraggled after the long drive. Much of the time the windows have been open as the drive was long and hot and the truck is not equipped with air-conditioning. Indeed, on our eventual return to the gleaming marble foyer of the Minshan hotel, the other immaculately dressed guests give us a wide berth, keen not to be contaminated by the cloud of dust which floats in the air around us. As we wait for the keys to our room, a cleaner appears and whisks over the marble floor behind us with a soft brush, removing all traces of our walk to the reception desk.

A BEWILDERING ARRAY OF GOODS FOR SALE.

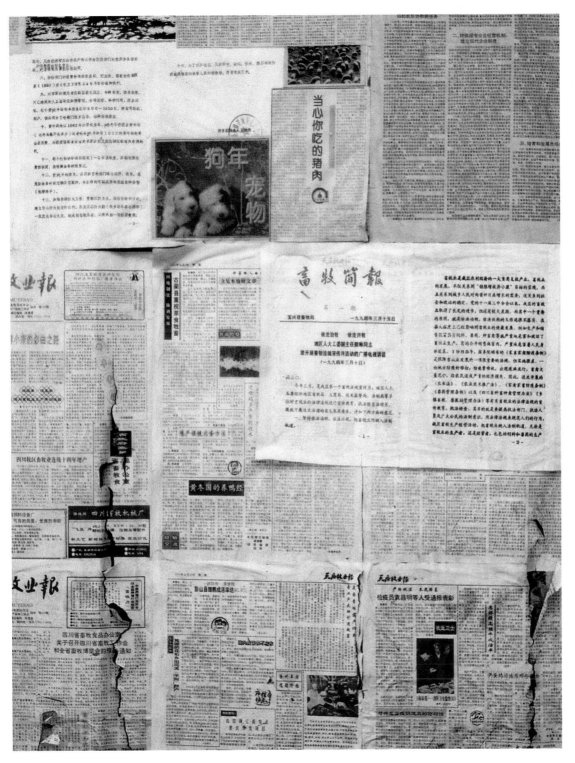

丙子流年事歉大利東西不利南方

太歲壓罡 乙酉甲午癸卯壬子辛酉庚午六生人下葬時宜避之便吉

是年三煞在南五黃占乾九巳丙午丁未戌乾亥八山忌用餘各山俱利

丙子納音屬水歲名郭嘉 歲德屬火歲德合在壬 歲支德屬辛

分龍 初伏 中伏 末伏

			用事土王
五月初九日	六月廿七日	五月初五日	二月初三日
六月廿七日		六月廿七日	六月十五日
			九月初九日

地母經 地母日 春社 秋社

春秋多雨水 桑葉無人要 青女多淹盤 黃龍土內盤 化成蝴蝶起 高田半成實 低下麥後美 魯齊五穀美 楚五穀

五穀憂鼠耗 豆麥半中收 蠶娘空房坐 先喜後還貴 絲綿綢絹貴 稅賦急啾啾

二月初四日 八月初六日

Chapter Seven

T 大熊猫

HE ancient city of Chengdu is believed to have been founded more than 2,300 years ago. Like most Chinese cities it has had a turbulent history. Chengdu began to thrive during the Qin Dynasty (221 - 226 BC) after China was unified as one empire. From that date it has always been linked with arts, crafts and cultural activities. By the tenth century it had also achieved great commercial importance – it was here that the first form of paper money was introduced.

The city's modern name, Chengdu, translates as 'perfect metropolis'. A population of two and a half million inhabit the capital and almost four times this number live in the surrounding metropolitan area.

Day Eight

We have a day in Chengdu to gather our energies before embarking on the long drive to Fentengxiao, the second destination in our quest to find giant pandas for Pollyanna to study and paint.

Daphne suggests that we may like to visit the hospital of traditional Chinese medicine for a restorative massage. The hospital is located at the edge of the city in a modern concrete building – an inappropriate home for practitioners of such ancient skills. As long ago as 2838 BC Shen Nong, a teacher of traditional medicine, had catalogued 365 medicinal herbs, tasting the majority of them himself, despite the risk of accidental poisoning. Many of his discoveries still hold good. Today's practitioners of herbal medicine are the custodians of a vast store of pharmaceutical and medicinal knowledge which has yet to be extensively studied and exploited in the West.

We are taken up in a lift to the top floor of the hospital. We are shown into a waiting-room and brought glasses of hot medicinal tea to drink before the massage. The tea is the shade of pink peculiar to dentist's mouthwash, but has a very pleasant fresh herbal taste. It is also very hot, and I have only managed to drink a couple of mouthfuls when Daphne returns to introduce me to the nurse who will be my masseuse. The nurse does not speak English, so Daphne briefly translates my specific aches and pains and then leaves us to communicate by sign language.

永

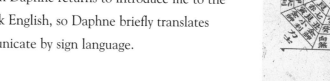

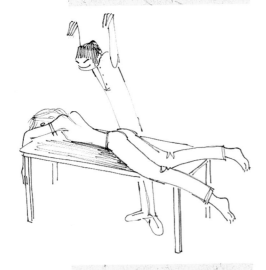

CHINESE MEDICINE
Traditional Chinese medicine is based on the use of herbs, acupuncture and a healthy diet. In its simplest form it is based on the belief that a person becomes ill when the two opposing forces of Yin and Yang become unbalanced within the body. The prescribed cures are intended to re-channel these natural energies, and thus ensure the recovery of the patient.

Medicinal herbs have been used in various forms in China for around 4,000 years. In the 16th century a respected doctor, Li Shizan, listed 11,000 prescriptions based on the use of nearly 2,000 herbs in his book the *Bencau Gangmu*. He had bravely tested many of these remedies on himself.

Many herbs are also used in day to day home cooking, often in nutritious soups – a far-sighted form of preventative medicine. Chinese people are often less concerned with the taste of a dish than with the long-term effects on their health.

The nurse beckons me to follow and we walk together down a corridor to a treatment room. I follow her in. There is a large desk in the centre of the room, behind which sits a doctor, evidently in the middle of a consultation with a patient. I assume we have the wrong room and am backing out of the door with a series of what I hope are apologetic hand gestures, when the nurse grabs my arm and pulls me back in. She points to a narrow bench at the back of the room and signals for me to lie down. I pause. This would seem to be something of an intrusion into the first occupant's privacy, even allowing for the fact that I do not understand Chinese. It would also seem to be a slight invasion of my privacy, as I had assumed I would need to disrobe for the massage and had not expected company.

I launch into a complex mime to try and convey some of these points. The nurse becomes understandably impatient at this piece of theatre and motions that I lie down fully dressed. She begins to massage my face and scalp with a firm but pleasant motion. It is very relaxing, but having understood through Daphne that my treatment is to last for around an hour, I am starting to wonder how I will feel after having my head massaged for sixty minutes. Suddenly the nurse delivers a series of sharp blows to the top of my thighs. I nearly fall off the bench in shock. I am also very relieved not to have undressed for the treatment – at least I have a layer of denim to offer me some protection. The nurse may be around five feet tall and very slim, but she can deliver blows like a sledgehammer. She turns me over to attend to my back, then two other nurses join her. They begin a conversation, punctuated by one or another of them leaning down and manipulating one of my limbs seemingly at random. One nurse leaves, but a few minutes later a fourth arrives to have a go. As I lie there a steady stream of people wander in and out of the room. Some approach and look at me, or join in briefly with my massage, others pass through briskly, intent on other duties.

For the final part of the massage I am physically sat upright on a low stool. A somewhat glazed looking Pollyanna rejoins me and is told to sit beside me. Daphne wanders in to watch, and to translate some of the nurse's comments. They are apparently marvelling at the length of my arms and legs, and also at the cast-iron knots of tension around my shoulder blades – presumably the result of the previous day's journey over potholes and trenches. More medicinal tea is brought and the treatment is over. I do in fact feel much fitter, and surprisingly refreshed.

永

By this stage the doctor, who is still sitting at his desk at the far side of the room, has finished his consultation with his previous patient. Daphne asks if we would like to meet him, and we are led over and introduced. Dr Ma Zhi Xiang is one of the most respected senior doctors in the hospital; he has just been invited over to Canada to give a series of lectures on the art of traditional Chinese medicine. We chat generally, with Daphne interpreting as usual, about the differences between Oriental and Western medicine. The medicine practised by Dr Ma Zhi Xiang has been developed over 3,000 years, and some of the herbal remedies have remained practically unchanged for centuries. Though he has some respect for more modern medicine, the doctor expresses his strong reservations about the widespread use of drugs and their unpleasant side effects. He tells us that none of the remedies used in herbalism has any side effects. The Chinese also take a much more holistic view of illness, treating the whole body and mind, rather than concentrating on specific symptoms. Even their general attitude to food reflects this approach, with dishes often being selected for their health giving properties rather than their taste.

The majority of the remedies prescribed in Chinese herbal medicine are derived from plants, herbs and roots. The doctor was aware of campaigning in the West aimed at ending the cruel practices which are used to obtain some of the animal products used in traditional medicine – including the barbaric treatment of Asiatic moon bears. Doctors are now encouraged to replace these ingredients with plant-based products which have a similar effect. Fortunately, there is no history of the giant panda being hunted for use in Chinese medicine. However, it has been recorded that drinking a glass of panda urine will dissolve a swallowed needle. How the herbalists reached this conclusion is a matter for much conjecture.

Dr Ma Zhi Xiang, who I am sure would not recommend this course of action in any circumstance, offers to give us a general consultation. I am wary, imagining that he will immediately tell me that I have six months left, but Pollyanna agrees with alacrity. The doctor asks her to hold out her right hand. He leans over and looks at her palm, barely touching her hand, but tapping the ends of her fingers lightly. Sitting back, he lists a catalogue of ailments from present muscle stiffness, to past illnesses and operations, including the removal of her appendix

阝 a hill . . .　今 people under a roof . . .　云 a cloud . . .　**YIN**

阝 a hill . . .　旦 sun above the horizon . . .　勿 rays of light, moving energy . . .　**YANG**

Yin and Yang are the Chinese symbols of complementary duality. Inherent in all substance, they constantly act and react upon each other. Yin is dark, negative and feminine, Yang is motion, the sun, masculine. Different aspects of one system, they can be seen in everything around us. When light falls on an object there is both illumination and shadow. The Chinese characters used to represent Yin and Yang portray the effect of the light of the sun on a mountain, one side cast in shadow, the other bathed in light.

... HE CAN DIAGNOSE OVER SEVEN HUNDRED ILLNESSES JUST BY EXAMINING A PATIENT'S HAND ...

HERBS COMMONLY USED IN HERBAL MEDICINE

Guo Qu Zi (*Wolfberry*)
Used in the treatment of diabetes, and to improve failing eyesight

Sheng Ma (*Bugbane*) Used in the treatment of the common cold, measles, and for the relief of some kinds of headache

Sheng Yao (*Chinese yam*)
Used to treat fatigue, or lack of appetite

Shang Zhi (*Mulberry wood*)
Used to treat high blood pressure, and for the relief of rheumatic pain

Zhu Liy (*An umbellate fungus*)
Used as a diuretic

nearly twenty years earlier. Pollyanna is stunned. Everything he describes is accurate; there are no assumptions or guesses which do not apply to her. Dr Ma Zhi Xiang tells us that he can diagnose over seven hundred illnesses just by examining a patient's hand, and can also tell their entire medical history, including operations and injuries. I am greatly impressed, but still nervous, more so since he has pin-pointed the state of Pollyanna's health with such unerring accuracy. He is bound to take one look at my palm and turn away shaking his head in sorrow.

Nervously, I stretch out my hand. He has barely glanced at it when his hand goes to the small of his back, indicating precisely the location of the pulled muscle in my back. Strained two months earlier, while I was working on an exhibition stand, it is still giving me some considerable pain. He followed this by a demonstration of the pain I am suffering in my right leg from the resulting pressure on the sciatic nerve. I am already impressed, but there is more to come. He tells me I suffer from an occasional ache in my lower left wisdom tooth, but that I have no pain there at the moment. This is also entirely accurate, though it has been pain free for around four months. Each diagnosis he gives is not only correct but located with complete precision. I look at my hand with a new respect, I had no idea that so much information was located there. He can even see trends towards future illnesses (for example, my left eye is slightly weaker than the right), and also any emotional or psychological problems.

Having previously only had experience of English hospitals and doctors, I am amazed not only by Dr Ma Zhi Xiang's methods of diagnosis, but also by the fact that people are constantly drifting in and out of the room during the consultations. Nurses, other doctors, even patients all wander in and out. Even Mr Jing joins us and sits on the edge of the desk to be given the news that I sometimes suffer painful periods.

We leave the hospital with a new found respect for Chinese medicine.

After grabbing a quick lunch in a street-side café, Daphne asks us if we would like to visit the opera house that afternoon to watch a performance. We both think this to be a marvellous idea, but we would need to return to the hotel to change, as we are still in jeans and shirts. She dismisses our concerns with a toss of her head and we drive to the theatre.

The opera house is set deep in the heart of the oldest part of Chengdu, and we pass between narrow lanes of overhanging wooden houses, barely wide enough for the truck. The streets here are thronging with people, cycling, walking, talking. Old men crouch on the street corners playing mah jong. The shops are competing with market stalls set up directly outside. Every other building seems to be a traditional tea house, full of regular clients, their chairs spilling out of the open doors onto the pavements. Above the street-level shop fronts are flats, each with a line of freshly washed clothing hanging outside the windows. All the garments are turned inside out, to prevent the right side of the fabric getting coated with the ever present dust from the street.

We reach the theatre, a large old building set back from the street front; the courtyard outside is filled with row upon row of identical bicycles. Daphne consults a hand-written notice pinned up front of house. She informs us that the afternoon's performance has been in progress for nearly an hour. With undeniable logic she then announces that this is of no importance, as we will not be able to understand a word of the plot.

We buy tickets and slip into the back of the theatre. The room is huge and very full. There is no circle or balcony; the stalls area is packed with individual chairs, arranged loosely into rows around a centre isle. All the seats appear to be taken, so we stand quietly against the back wall. Suddenly, we are spotted by the manageress of the theatre, a smiling, plump lady, swathed in floral fabric, she advances. We are visitors, we cannot possibly stand at the back. We protest in hushed whispers that there is no need to go to any trouble, we are fine, really, but she seizes Pollyanna by the arm and marches us down the centre isle towards the stage. Reaching the front row, she unceremoniously throws a couple of elderly Chinese gentlemen out of their seats. We try to protest (quietly since the performance is in full swing a few feet away from us), but she will have none of it. They live in Chengdu, they can visit the opera any time, next week, the week after, the week after that. We will have returned home by then, this is our only opportunity. We meekly sit down, knees crushed against the front of the stage. A minute or so later, the manageress returns, bearing two mugs of tea which she places on the edge of the stage in front of us. Looking along, we can see that in front of the footlights the stage is ringed with a row of mugs, flasks and jars – most of the audience have brought some refreshment with them. All the cups and mugs we have used on our journey so far have had lids, and these are no exception. They are useful not only for keeping the drink hot, but also for keeping the liquid dust free. Many

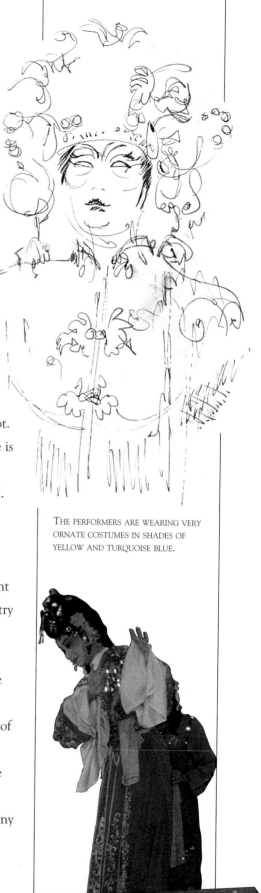

THE PERFORMERS ARE WEARING VERY
ORNATE COSTUMES IN SHADES OF
YELLOW AND TURQUOISE BLUE.

Actors from Opera –
Costumes vivid colours –
silks/feathers/beadwork
faces: painted masks
Movements highly
defined & theatrical

of the people out on the streets, and in the theatre, drink from empty jam jars, retaining the screw lids to protect their tea.

We finally turn our attention to the stage. It is practically bare of scenery, except for a plain backcloth, two desks and a large chair centre stage. The performers are wearing very ornate costumes in shades of yellow and turquoise blue, and there appear to be several men dressed as women, and women dressed as men. There are six performers currently singing, the sound of their voices unlike anything I have previously heard. The music is very complex, voices singing in different rhythms, layered on top of one another, interspersed with long swooping solos. Daphne tells us that the Chinese opera, the most popular form of theatre in the days of Imperial China, is now a dying art form. Most of the pieces performed are over two hundred years old, and it takes up to seven years of training to perfect the singing technique .

She attempts briefly to explain the plot of the opera we are currently watching. It is a historical piece, based loosely on fact. Two real-life presidents are arguing over possession of land (as usual). The goodie is from the area which is now Chengdu, the baddie is from a neighbouring province which no longer exists. The baddie is dressed as a woman, in order to present him as a figure of ridicule (works every time). He is wearing a floor-length blue dress, full make up and an elaborate wig and head-dress. Confusingly, the other president, who is not dressed as a woman, is wearing a floor-length yellow dress, full make up and a high wig, decorated with feathers. His consort, a women who I am lead to understand is playing a male court official, also sports a natty line in head gear, topped off with a four-foot-long pheasant tail feather.

scarlet & yellow
silks, tassels
peacock feathers
embroidery/beads

Although archaic Mandarin is completely unintelligible to us, we find that, to a point, we can follow the plot. The movements around the set and the sound of the music clearly conveys to us the emotion of the piece, and we can follow the train of arguments and reconciliations. We realise that there is also a surprising amount of humour within the plot – generated largely by the baddie's mincing progress around the stage. This humour is much appreciated by the rest of the audience.

Briefly distracted by our progress down the isle, they have now turned their attention back to the stage and are roaring with laughter at every joke. They repeat each funny line several times to each other, loudly discussing the finer points with their neighbours. They keep up a running commentary on the plot, talking, laughing, smoking, drinking tea and spitting on the floor. The theatre is full of noise and movement but the performers continue unfazed on the stage.

Stage left, through the inadequate side curtains, we can clearly see the 'orchestra' – four musicians surrounded by a range of unidentifiable instruments which they pick up and play in turn. When the singers have an unaccompanied segment, the orchestra down instruments, light cigarettes and wander round at the side of the stage slurping tea and spitting. Also in full view behind them are the four actors preparing for the next section of the afternoon's entertainment. We can see them applying thick stage make up, using a cracked full-length mirror leaning against the wall, arranging and adjusting costumes and balancing towering head-dresses on top of wigs.

The second piece is a completely new story. I am not clear if everyone in the first piece lived happily ever after, Daphne having wandered off at that point. Performance number two turns out to be a variation on the theme of *Romeo and Juliet*, with the added twist that Romeo wears a floor-length peacock blue dress and scarlet lip gloss. Additional excitement is created when both the young lovers metamorphose into butterflies at the end.

At this point we leave. Although the music is not easy on the ear, I am entranced by the spectacle, and would happily have stayed for the rest of the day. However, there are another three operas still to follow and apparently it is common for members of the audience to stay for one or two then leave. Much of the audience is made up of older people; Daphne tells us that they will probably visit each time the theatre is opened; perhaps two or three times a week.

We walk from the theatre to a tea house on the opposite side of the street, and sit back with bowls of fresh tea, to watch the world go by. The tea is served to us with some degree of ceremony. The china bowls are carried to us on a tray and the fresh green leaves dropped in at the table. A gleaming copper kettle of boiling water follows, the bowls are filled and the ornate lids replaced. When I remove my lid a few moments later to peer in and give the tea a quick stir, it is taken from my hand and gently but firmly replaced. It is good tea and I must wait for it to reach its full strength

in its own time. As in the theatre most of the clients at the tables here are elderly. Many of them have brought their pet caged birds with them – finches and canaries – and they twitter and flutter in their shiny bamboo cages hanging from the rafters above us. Daphne tells us that the other patrons are sitting round reminiscing about the old days – and I wish more than ever that I could understand the language.

On leaving the tea house we pause at a narrow dusty shop selling traditional Chinese artists' materials. Pollyanna is captivated by the beauty of the brushes and inks used by artists and calligraphers. The most basic of utensils are displayed on ornate stands or immaculately arranged

THE TEA IS SERVED TO US WITH SOME DEGREE OF CEREMONY.

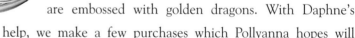

in cloth-covered boxes, giving them the status of works of art in their own right. Sets of brushes made from white goat hair taper gracefully to a rounded point, the inner core waxed to make them springy and flexible. The water bowls are decorated with delicate landscapes or images of tigers and exotic birds. Even the blocks of inks, destined to be ground down and mixed with water, are embossed with golden dragons. With Daphne's help, we make a few purchases which Pollyanna hopes will prove inspirational when she is back in her Derbyshire studio.

In choosing to paint Chinese landscapes and wildlife, she is following in a respected and long established tradition. Artistic creation has long been highly prized in China, with the skills of calligraphy, poetry and painting known as 'the three perfections'.

In the evening we are to eat in 'the most beautiful restaurant in all of Chengdu' according to Daphne. Resembling a temple more than a restaurant, it lives up to her description. Small roofs of golden scalloped tiles at different levels cover high doorways leading into a succession of rooms of varying sizes arranged around a central open-air courtyard. We are given a small private

dining-room, looking out onto the formal pool at the centre. There are plants everywhere: set in tubs, at the centre of the tables, in hanging baskets, even trailing down from the roofs. The food is also of exceptional quality. A dazzlingly large array of dishes is brought to the table, including many traditional recipes. We sample for the first time the intriguingly named

'pock-marked Grandmother Chen's bean curd', a dish of tofu in a delicious chilli-based sauce. This dish is still made to a traditional recipe, prepared and cooked in exactly the same way as it was by Grandmother Chen herself when she ran an inn in the city some two hundred years ago.

After the meal, we make our way back to the considerably newer comforts of our hotel, having finally devised a method of crossing Chengdu's terrifying roads. The largest busiest roads carry four or five lanes of traffic in each direction. There are pedestrian crossings at intervals, but these are completely ignored by the vehicles which move at a steady speed and are not prepared to make an inconvenient interruption to their journey just to avoid a pedestrian. The inhabitants of the city do not wait for a gap in the traffic, they simply step off the kerb and weave their way through the lanes of vehicles, pausing only to avoid the cyclists who are tracing their own random courses between the buses and cars.

After making a couple of abortive attempts to cross on a crossing, only to be driven back in terror to the edge of the pavement, I put my new plan into action. I wait for some residents of Chengdu to cross and then cross with them. I walk, not behind them, where I would be flattened under the wheels of the truck they have just narrowly avoided, but parallel to them, attached as if by an invisible cord to their elbow. Thus, in formation, we move through the narrow gaps between the lanes of traffic, arriving safely on the opposite side of the road.

The plan works and eventually we reach the hotel in safety. Before retiring to bed we unpack and re-pack, organising ourselves for the second part of our quest to find the giant panda.

HOT SICHUAN TOFU WITH MUSHROOMS

Serves 4

3 - 4 small Chinese dried mushrooms
3 cakes tofu
fi tsp of finely chopped garlic
1 leek, sliced
1 tbsp black bean sauce
1 tbsp soy sauce
1 tsp chilli bean sauce
4 tbsp water
2 tsp cornflour
fi tsp sesame oil
fi tsp of salt
Black pepper

Step 1
Soak the Chinese mushrooms in warm water for 30 minutes. Drain and squeeze mushrooms to extract as much of the moisture as possible. Cut off any hard stems and discard. Thinly slice mushrooms.

Step 2
Cut the tofu into cubes approximately 1cm deep, bring some water to the boil in a small wok, add the tofu and blanch for approximately 3 minutes. Remove and drain well.

Step 3
Heat the oil in a pre-heated wok. Add the mushrooms, chopped leek, salt and sauces and stir well for approximately 1 minute.

Step 4
Add the water, followed by the tofu. Bring to the boil and simmer for approximately 2 minutes.

Step 5
Add the cornflour to thicken. Sprinkle with sesame oil and black pepper and serve piping hot.

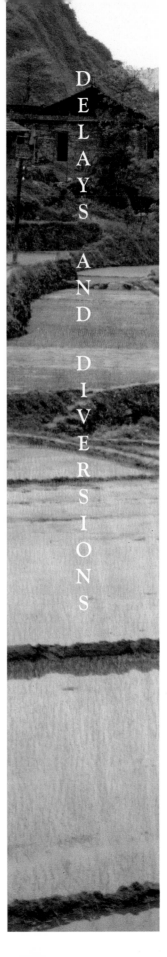

Chapter Eight

C 大熊猫 HINA has had a turbulent political history. At various times this century travel has been severely restricted, if not prohibited entirely. Since the early seventies, however, the country has become progressively more open and accessible to tourists and business people alike. In many areas the potential for tourism has been widely developed. Understandably most visitors have headed for the same destinations – the more accessible parts of the Great Wall, or sites of historical or cultural significance, such as Xi'an, home of the terracotta army. In most major cities, including Chengdu, huge Western-style hotels have been built, and many restaurants have menus printed in English.

It came as something of a surprise to us, when trying to plan our journey, to discover that large areas of the country are still out of bounds to foreigners. On our arrival it also became clear that some of the wilder regions, which can be freely visited, still remain largely unexplored. Business is conducted in the cities, and once off the beaten track there are no provisions for tourists. The vast tracts of farmland and countryside often do not contain any major landmarks or exceptional attractions to make the long uncomfortable drives on rough roads worthwhile.

While researching the expedition we had been told of the work being done in a hospital for sick pandas in the Fentengxiao reserve, and were keen to visit. We were told by the Chinese Embassy that this would be possible. The areas we would need to travel through had been officially designated 'open' to Western visitors eight months before we were due to arrive. We did not realise until we made our journey that this did not necessarily mean that any Westerners had chosen to go.

Day Nine

We meet Daphne and Mr Jing outside the Minshan hotel at 6.00 am and set off once again through the suburbs of Chengdu. Initially we are travelling in the same direction as Wolong. Geographically the two reserves are quite close, but separated by a high mountain range. The reserve of Fentengxiao is further from the city and less easily accessible. Mr Jing has estimated that it will take us the best part of two days to drive there.

Daphne has never travelled out to this area before. Nor, it emerges, has Mr Jing. The Chengdu branch of the Chinese International Travel Service, the bureau which employs them both, has never before been asked to provide a driver or interpreter to accompany clients to our destination. Daphne has been instructed to keep a careful record of all the inns in which we stay en route, the restaurants we frequent and the places we visit for the company's future reference.

As we head away from the city, the traffic on the road gradually thins out, but the driving seems to deteriorate. Drivers go faster and are more reckless than in the centre of Chengdu.

There are a lot of near misses, and we express our surprise that there are not more road accidents. We spoke too soon. Within the next two and half hours we pass at least half a dozen. We see a van which has unwisely driven into the side of a police car; a lorry crashed into a streetlight, now lying across the road with exposed wires sparking on the tarmac; a truck overturned in a ditch; a lorry sideways across the road with the cab through the wall of a house. Miraculously, none of the crashes seems to have caused any serious injuries, and at each one groups of people have gathered to watch as the drivers attempt to right their vehicles. The locals appear to regard the crashes as diversions laid on for their entertainment, and heckle or shout encouragement. Groups of small childen run out to play, laughing and shouting on the overturned trucks.

At some stages, the road is entirely blocked and we are held up for considerable lengths of time. If we step out of the vehicle we attract the usual attention for looking spectacularly foreign and quickly become far more interesting to the local people than the mangled vehicles by the roadside. At five feet ten inches, we tower over the men, as well as the women. Our extremely pale complexions are the colour of plain yoghurt; our blonde hair is the finishing touch to help us draw

POLLYANNA USES HER FOUNTAIN PEN TO CAPTURE, IN SIMPLE LINES, THE CHARACTER IN EACH FACE.

AT FIVE FEET TEN INCHES, WE TOWER OVER THE MEN, AS WELL AS THE WOMEN.

attention to ourselves. The real fascination for most of the Chinese people we meet, however, is the colour of our eyes. Even if they have occasionally seen blonde hair, few of them have met people with blue or grey eyes. I often find the people I am talking to intently staring into my eyes, watching the movement of the pupils, which is all a little unnerving. Pollyanna is as interested in the Chinese people as they are fascinated by us and she quickly fills her sketch pad with drawings of the people we encounter.

After driving for around six hours we have covered remarkably little ground due to all the delays. We are saddle sore and hungry, so we stop in a small town to find a restaurant. The restaurant is small, but extremely good. The speciality of the house is brought to our table first – one of the ironed ducks we have seen hanging from market stalls, but not yet sampled. It is lying, complete with head and beak, on a bed of cooked lettuce, drizzled with a spicy honey sauce. Other dishes arrive, including a wide range of largely unfamiliar vegetables. We recognise a flat green pepper and spring onions, but the rest are a mystery. We are told that they are mainly wild plants picked freshly that morning. For the first time since our arrival we are served pudding – a dish of set ground rice sprinkled with sugar. Not overtly sweet, it is eaten in tandem with the rest of the food.

At the end of the meal I ask if I could possibly visit the ladies. No. They do not have a toilet here. But, a little way across the town there is a very good public lavatory, it is very clean, but, because of the high standard, it is necessary to pay. We set off. We cross three roads, then a large muddy field. We find the toilet, we pay our money as instructed to the formidable female attendant sitting behind a sturdy trestle table, guarding the convenience with her arms resolutely folded. There is one small hut for the ladies, and we assume that it will contain one squat loo, similar to the others we have seen previously. I go in. I freeze. Rather than one loo, there is in front of me a trench dug into the ground, divided into four by low walls. These mini cubicles have no doors (and indeed very little in the way of sides, since the walls are only a metre high). There are three women already making use of the facilities. As I walk in they are chatting casually, but when they see me, they also freeze. They have stopped dead because an alien has walked into the loo; I am rooted to the spot because I have to use the lavatory (well, the trench) **in front of people.** I suddenly feel very English. We are all startled out of our trance-like frozen

THE SPECIALITY OF THE HOUSE IS BROUGHT TO OUR TABLE FIRST – ONE OF THE IRONED DUCKS WE HAVE SEEN HANGING FROM MARKET STALLS, BUT NOT YET SAMPLED.

state when one of the women leaps up, grabs her skirts and flees outside as fast as she can. I consider taking a deep breath, but remember where I am, so cough discreetly instead, and walk to the other side of the furthest low partition, nearest the wall. Dilemma. I am too tall to lower my jeans with any semblance of decency under cover of the low wall. The other women cast side-long glances at the strange pantomime which follows. I try to distract myself by watching a cockroach walking along the floor in front of my feet. (The restaurant owner's definition of clean evidently does not coincide with mine.) Deciding not to visit the kitchens on my return, I leave, walking past my audience back to the restaurant, with as much dignity as I can muster.

We are running so far behind schedule because of the morning's delays that it seems unlikely that we will be able to reach Baoxin county, our first intended stopping point, by evening. Daphne is concerned that if we drive much further into the countryside we will not be able to find any inns in the remote villages on the way to Baoxin, so we decide not to cover too much ground but to make a diversion to Bahzang lake, which the restaurant owner assures us is a famous local beauty spot, about an hour's drive away.

Unfortunately, by the time we arrive the weather, already dull and grey, has deteriorated. So much for the rains only happening at night. We walk down a long series of steps and platforms to the edge of the lake, getting more and more soggy with each level. At the water's edge Daphne launches into a series of complex negotiations and hires us a motor boat, complete with driver. We are here, we **will** see the lake. The inside of the boat is even soggier than we are, despite having the cover of a roof. The walls inside the boat are decorated with a surprising choice of green flowered linoleum. A pink plastic carnation stuck into the top of the windshield adds to the ambience, but is less use to us than a windscreen wiper, which the boat does not possess. Within a few minutes of leaving the shore the driver's line of vision is completely obscured by spray. This is a little unsettling, as the lake is full of traffic: fishing boats; motor boats; pleasure cruisers; coracles; even small house boats, or rather floating shacks with television aerials sticking up from the roofs. I am starting to calculate the odds of swimming back to the bank after an unnecessarily wet accident, when the driver opens the side window, lowers a pink plastic bucket into the water, fills it with water and hurls the contents at the windshield, thus clearing it. Unfortunately, there is a gap of several centimetres between the base of the glass and the edge of the boat, so each time he repeats this procedure he is completely drenched from the waist down. We cruise sedately

MISTY WATERS
IN THE COLLECTION OF MR & MRS M HAYNES
(UK)

around the lake, which I have on good authority is surrounded by spectacular views and is very beautiful, but I cannot confirm this, as a very heavy fog has descended and visibility is down to approximately a metre. Objects occasionally loom damply towards us out of the gloom and we valiantly photograph them before they recede back into the mists once more.

There is a fairly large island rising from the centre of the lake. This comes as a surprise, for we are aware of it only when we have almost crashed onto the rocks at the base. Mooring the boat, we step out onto dryish land and climb up the flights of stone stairs towards the top of the hill. There are two small temples on the island, a few parties of wet local tourists and an ornamental fish pond. We peer in, full of hope, but it is green and slimy, with not a koi carp in sight. We circle the island, seeing all the available sights, including the gents' loos, due to a slight mix up with the Chinese characters, and then search hopefully for a cup of tea. There is indeed a small café, and we find Daphne and Mr Jing already comfortably installed in front of the karaoke machine. Karaoke is extremely popular in China, but we had not expected to find a bar on an island no more than two kilometres wide. We join them for a welcome cup of hot tea, and Daphne proceeds to entertain us. We soon discover that she has a wonderful singing voice. When questioned she admits that she used to sing professionally, to earn money while at university. She sings Cantonese and Japanese pop songs, while lots of pretty Oriental girls, sitting under trees and floating down rivers in rowing boats, drift across the video screens behind her. For our benefit she then performs a selection of traditional Chinese songs in Mandarin, accompanied by pictures of floating lotus blossoms. After a little encouragement Mr Jing also sings for us, his enthusiasm more than compensating for any lack of vocal skills. Fortunately for all concerned the machine is not equipped with any tapes of English songs, so we are unable to reciprocate.

The boat returns us to the mainland and we drive back to Ya'an, the closest sizeable town. The fog is still very thick, even away from the shores of the lake, and we are glad that we took the decision not to press on to Baoxin. We are to spend the night in the largest hotel in town. A board outside informs Daphne that Western breakfast is served, news which she passes on to us with great delight. Despite this lure, the hotel has evidently attracted few Western visitors. The receptionist has seldom seen foreigners, and is overcome with confusion. Having shown us up three flights of echoing concrete stairs to our room, she discovers that she has omitted to bring the key with her, so she goes all the way back down to her desk to fetch it. Once in, we inspect

... A CANDLELIT BANQUET APPEARS
AS IF BY MAGIC. A WHOLE FISH,
CAUGHT FRESHLY FROM THE RIVER
THAT MORNING ...
BELOW: ... A SPECTACULAR
TRADITIONAL SICHUAN DISH ...

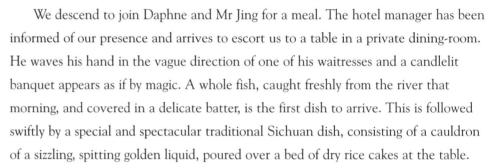

our quarters. The bedroom is basic, but quite reasonable. There is even a portable television perched on a shelf in the corner but, as the town is currently experiencing a power cut, we are unable to test it.

A door in one corner leads to the bathroom. We peer in but, without the benefit of electric light, cannot make out the full extent of the facilities. The small high window does not cast much light on the situation, but we are relieved to see a sit-down loo. The bath tub contains a blackened slimy mop propped up at one end, but there seems to be a shower fitting. As my eyes adjust to the gloom, I can also make out the black dirt-encrusted crack stretching right across the width of the hand basin. There is dirt banked up in the corners of the room, and a selection of fag ends on the floor in front of the toilet. I console myself with the fact that it will all probably look brighter when the power is restored.

We descend to join Daphne and Mr Jing for a meal. The hotel manager has been informed of our presence and arrives to escort us to a table in a private dining-room. He waves his hand in the vague direction of one of his waitresses and a candlelit banquet appears as if by magic. A whole fish, caught freshly from the river that morning, and covered in a delicate batter, is the first dish to arrive. This is followed swiftly by a special and spectacular traditional Sichuan dish, consisting of a cauldron of a sizzling, spitting golden liquid, poured over a bed of dry rice cakes at the table. The pale pink meat floating on the surface turns out, on closer investigation, to be spam; not, I suspect, the most traditional of ingredients. This is accompanied by cold cucumber in a hot sauce, pickled spring onions, slices of aubergine oozing with a garlic and chilli dressing, rice and long clear slippery noodles which are romantically named 'rain of the desert'. This feast is washed down with the best local beer, 'emperor's tea' and corn soup, a thin yellow liquid, which tastes a little like unsweetened custard. The manager bobs in and out every few minutes to ask if everything is to our satisfaction, and we assure him that everything is delicious. I am tempted to have a quiet word about the bathroom, but he has gone to so much trouble to please us, that I get the distinct impression that he would do the only honourable thing and commit suicide if he felt that the hotel had failed, so I refrain. At the end of the meal, he shyly asks if I would have a photograph taken with his waitresses. I agree, and they line up by the table. I stand and make my way over to join them. They scatter to the four corners of the room. Eventually the manager rounds them up again, and giggling and twittering they stand as close to me as they dare and a photograph is taken.

Outside the hotel a large number of pedicabs has gathered. These pedal-powered tricycles, with a seat to carry passengers, have largely replaced rickshaws in most areas of China. Daphne suggests that we hire one as it would be a charming way to see the town. I have a few qualms about being pedalled around by another human being, but Daphne manages to convince me that all the locals use them like taxis and I am worrying unnecessarily. We finally agree to take a tour, and then the haggling begins. Reassuring me was obviously the easy part. Daphne and one of the pedicab drivers enter into a frantic and furious discussion. Voices are raised and there is much arm waving and pointing. We stand by, smiling faintly. Thirty additional pedicabs, and a large group of spectators, gather to watch the proceedings; by the time a satisfactory price has been negotiated, the road is virtually blocked.

We battle our way through the throng, perched side by side on the seat at the back of the tricycle. We soon come to the conclusion that, although in theory this may be a delightful way to view a new place, in practice it is not without its problems. Firstly, we are extremely cramped. Like so many things in China the seats are not designed for people of our height. It is still raining and we are hunched over beneath the canopy hood. When the driver sits on the seat in front we are left with a minute gap to see the sights. Huddled together, we drive through the dark streets at a startling rate. Houses and shops flash past and a few small statues loom out of the rain. Many of the shops are still open; the barbers' shops appear to be doing a particularly roaring trade, even at eleven o'clock.

I cannot shake my negative feelings at being pedalled round by man power, despite the fact that our driver is evidently extremely strong. He shows barely any signs of exertion at any stage of the journey. Sitting behind him, on the other hand, I am agonising over every uphill inch. I am also gripped by panic over every downhill inch, as it soon becomes clear that we are not in

HUDDLED TOGETHER, WE DRIVE THROUGH THE DARK STREETS AT A STARTLING RATE.

TYPICAL CHINESE BREAKFAST.

possession of functioning brakes. We feel very vulnerable sitting on the back of this small and flimsy form of transport, especially when huge lorries thunder past us, our eyes barely level with the tops of their wheel arches. We overtake a tractor and race down a steep hill to drive the wrong way round a roundabout at the bottom. I shut my eyes. I open them again to find the ends of two long planks of wood poking into the cab, inches from my chest. We are riding behind a handcart, its precarious cargo overhanging the end by several metres, extending into a space which I am already occupying. I close my eyes again.

Back safely at the hotel, we undermine all of Daphne's careful haggling by massively overpaying the driver. He deserves every penny.

Joy! We have electric light! I rush into the bathroom and switch on the light. Cockroaches scuttle under the bath away from the unaccustomed glare. I rush out again. The single electric bulb suspended on a wire from the ceiling is indeed functioning, but it is green. Fairly dim, but very green, it was evidently provided by an itinerant fairground owner. If the cracked sink and general air of grime had seemed a little unsavoury in the gloom, under a green light the bathroom has the appearance of having materialised from an alien hell. I can now make out clearly the peeling cracked linoleum and the bowl of scum standing in the bath. The cigarette butts are tinged with a green glow. This is one scene that Pollyanna won't be recording in her sketch pad for posterity. I close the door gently behind me and have a little sit down on the edge of the bed.

As in all the hotel rooms we have visited in China, from the grandest to the most basic, we have been provided with two flasks of boiling water. Using this, I wash in the shallow tray the flasks are standing in and retire to bed, to sleep, perchance to dream of the bathroom in the Minshan hotel, in Chengdu, which, on our arrival, had a paper strip stretched across the toilet seat bearing the legend 'sterilised'.

Day Ten

Down to the dining-room for the famed Western breakfast. This consists of a bowl of sweetened yak's milk and a hard boiled egg served in a delicate china bowl with a pair of chopsticks. The star exhibit is a cup of coffee. We have not so far come across anybody drinking or serving coffee on our journey. After one sip, I understand why. Dark and strong, it is evil tasting and scarcely recognisable as coffee. The staff are standing round, proudly observing us, I smile weakly and tip the yak's milk into the cup in an attempt to dilute the foul beverage. The coffee lightens in colour a couple of degrees, but the taste is not improved. I eat a little of the egg and pick half-heartedly at Daphne's bowl of peanuts, but the bathroom appears to have stolen my appetite.

THE WESTERN BREAKFAST.

After breakfast, the manager and his entire staff gather at the entrance to wish us well on our journey. We make our way along the line, nodding, smiling and shaking hands, feeling all the while like a low budget version of royalty, until we are free to set off on the next stage of our trek, the good wishes of our host still ringing in our ears.

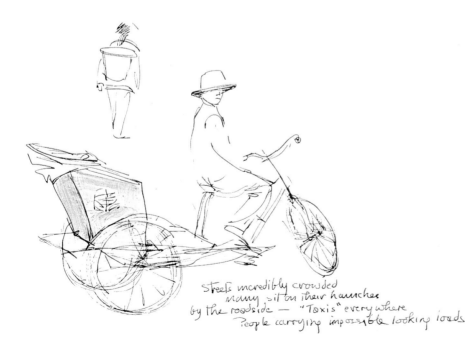

Streets incredibly crowded
many sit on their haunches
by the roadside — "Taxis" everywhere
People carrying impossible looking loads

Chapter Nine

B

大熊猫

AOXIN county became familiar to me through my reading and research before we flew to China. Père David was based there when he discovered the giant panda, while undertaking his historical journeys into the mountains studying and cataloguing the native wildlife. Without his dedicated work we would not have been making this journey of our own over a century later.

Armand David was a remarkable naturalist. Born in 1826, he entered the Catholic order of the Congregation of Lazarists at the age of twenty-two. He was ordained in 1856, and eleven years later was sent to Beijing to undertake missionary work. It had been his life-time ambition to carry out this work in China. In a letter to his superior written just two years after his ordination he wrote: 'I never stop dreaming at night about joining the Chinese mission. For the past twelve years I have thought of nothing else than working for the salvation of non-believers.'

As a child he had developed a fascination for the natural world and, encouraged by his father, a doctor, built up a large collection of native French insects, plants and birds. This interest was to stay with him into adulthood. During his time working in China he was to discover some of Asia's most remarkable flora and fauna, hitherto unknown to the Western world, including some fifty-eight species of birds and in excess of one hundred species of insects.

Many of the flowers he discovered carry his name to this day, as does the Père David's deer, an unusual splay-hoofed mammal, already extinct in the wild for over 1,500 years when Père David reached China. He discovered a captive herd in the emperor's imperial hunting ground and managed, at great personal risk, to obtain the remains of two of the deer for identification. He later arranged for the shipment of live animals back to Europe, where they began to breed. In 1894, long after Père David had left Beijing, a disastrous flood was to destroy most of the captive herd. Many of them were slaughtered for food by the peasants whose homes and livelihood had also been devastated by the flood. Years later the few remaining animals were killed during the Boxer Rebellion, and the species was completely wiped out in China. Fortunately, the

永

. . . THE PÈRE DAVID'S DEER, AN UNUSUAL SPLAY-HOOFED MAMMAL, ALREADY EXTINCT IN THE WILD FOR OVER 1,500 YEARS WHEN PÈRE DAVID REACHED CHINA. HE DISCOVERED A CAPTIVE HERD IN THE EMPEROR'S IMPERIAL HUNTING GROUND . . .

PHOTOS: CARE FOR THE WILD

few Père David's deer in the West continued to breed and thrive. In 1954, descendants of the original deer sent over by Père David were returned to Beijing for breeding. In 1985, a further nineteen were sent back to China. Without Père David's work the deer which bears his name would not have survived into the twentieth century.

His second stay in China lasted from 1867 to 1874, and brought him to Baoxing. In those days the journey from Chengdu involved six days of arduous travel.

From his base in a Catholic college, Père David explored the surrounding mountains. Returning from one such expedition, he was invited to rest at the home of Li, a wealthy landowner, and saw on his wall the skin of a 'white and black bear'. He described his discovery in a letter to Alphonse Milne-Edwards, son of the director of the Musée d'Histoire Naturelle in Paris, the eventual recipients of all the specimens collected on the epic journeys:

I would ask you to publish quickly the following brief description of a bear which appears to be new to science: very large, according to my hunters. Ears short. Hair fairly short, beneath the four feet very hairy.

Colours: white with the ears, the surroundings of the eyes, the tip of the tail and the four legs brownish black. The black on the fore legs is joined over the back in a straight band ... I have not seen this species which is easily the prettiest kind of animal I know in the museums of Europe; perhaps it is new to science!

Shortly afterwards, Père David's Christian hunters returned from the mountains bringing him a young panda, 'which they caught alive but unfortunately killed so it could be carried more easily'. From this he identified his 'new species of *ursus* (bear), very remarkable because of its colour, but also for its paws which are hairy underneath and for other characters.' Though he initially classified it as a bear, Père David was later to remark on a number of similarities between his discovery and the red panda.

Père David was a remarkable man who had a genuine love and respect for the animals he studied which went beyond scientific curiosity. Though he was willing to collect specimens in the name of science, and was a good shot with a rifle, he kept largely to a vegetarian diet. He records in his diaries: 'I observe the principle of never killing an animal not needed for my natural history collections. I find it less distressing to feed myself with rice or millet than to kill one of these poor creatures who revel in life so joyously and do not harm nature, but on the contrary embellish it. This attitude is not always agreeable to my servants, especially when it is a question of pheasants, but I hold firmly to my rule.'

Despite his continuing work in the mountains that ultimately brought his discovery to the attention of the West, Père David was never to see a live giant panda.

Day Ten Continues

Just a few miles out from Ya'an the roads deteriorate suddenly and dramatically. We are driving along a series of dirt tracks, often partially blocked by boulders or landslips, following the course of the Min river. The river runs through a spectacular gorge, ahead of us we can just make out the ridged line of the 'honey pot' mountains of the Tibetan borderlands, our destination. Within a few hours we begin to climb. I notice that every now and then Mr Jing stops to speak to people on the roadside, or at work in the fields. This is new, and I ask Daphne why he has suddenly developed an overwhelming desire to meet new people. There is a simple explanation. Mr Jing was unable to locate a map of the roads in this region before we set out. So, each time the road divides, he stops to ask the local people the direction of Baoxin town. It is only then that I realise I have not seen a single road sign since leaving the city. Most of the people using these roads are farmers, driving produce from one village to another, and the routes are familiar to them. The majority of the people who live in these remote villages will not travel more than a radius of twenty kilometres in their whole lives. Few city dwellers find reasons to travel this far into the countryside. We drive on, through

THE RIVER RUNS THROUGH A SPECTACULAR GORGE, AHEAD OF US WE CAN JUST MAKE OUT THE RIDGED LINE OF THE 'HONEY POT' MOUNTAINS OF THE TIBETAN BORDERLANDS, OUR DESTINATION.

acres of farmland, every inch of the land seems dedicated to producing food. The bushes of a tea plantation rise on either side of the track, row upon row of immaculate hedges. Workers with wicker baskets across their shoulders harvest the tiny tender green shoots from the tips of the bushes. Pollyanna's father was a tea and coffee dealer so we pull over to the edge and stop to watch for a while. This is the first time she has seen China tea growing. The tea pickers glance at us, but do not interrupt their labours. Huge straw hats shelter them from the sun as they work. Evidently this is a family concern for even the youngest children are out in the plantation helping with the tea gathering.

Baoxin turns out to be further from Ya'an than any of us had anticipated. The pitted and potholed roads have again made for a slow and uncomfortable day's travelling. It is very late when we arrive in the town; we are all over tired and Mr Jing, who has been driving since early morning, looks exhausted.

Daphne, Pollyanna and I have all dozed fitfully towards the end of the afternoon, only to be rudely jolted awake as the vehicle clatters over another series of potholes.

The county town of Baoxin is smaller than I expected. Built on a hill, there is one main street, lined with square concrete housing. There is one hostel at the top of the street, and this is where we are to stay overnight. The management looks at us with suspicion. They are not sure if they should accommodate foreigners. We produce our passports for inspection, along with sheaves of papers, visas and passes. Daphne, normally patient and tolerant, is tired and fractious. Eventually they agree to put us up for the night, though they do not appear thrilled at the

Tea in 'hedges

leaves picked & dropped into loose woven baskets at waist.

whole families appear to be at work picking the tea leaves.

prospect. We crawl up the stairs to our room and collapse for the night. The whole party of four is too tired to find anywhere to eat out. Daphne buys some fruit from a roadside stall and we eat it in our rooms, along with our emergency pack of biscuits, purchased in Chengdu.

There are many small stalls on the street below our window; the local people selling their surplus goods which are not already contracted to the state. Crates of apples and oranges, chillies and peppers, stand beside clusters of squawking chickens. A row of long thin cuts of unidentifiable meat hangs between two metal poles, unprotected from the dust, flies and traffic fumes. We watch as a local woman makes a selection, prodding firmly at the joint of her choice. A price agreed, the meat is unhooked and flung unwrapped over the handlebars of her bicycle.

Our room in the hostel comes as a pleasant surprise after the frosty welcome. It is reasonably clean, furnished with two single beds and a wicker chair. Ornate sequinned and embroidered pillowcases sit at the top of each bed, glittering but grimy, and very purple floor-length curtains hang at the window. Worn out by the drive, we do not have the strength to explore further. I am asleep before my head has touched the fuchsia sequins.

Day Eleven

We are woken at 6.30 am by a cockerel crowing with unnecessary vigour in the street below. I open my eyes to find my field of vision filled entirely by the very purple curtains. I notice that they appear to have a random pattern of small back dots, which seem to be leaping about in front of my eyes. Slowly I realise that the black dots really are jumping. The very purple curtains have fleas.

We meet Daphne and Mr Jing for breakfast at 9.30 am. This is a much later start than originally scheduled, but we were all too much in need of sleep to be ready for 7.00 am as originally planned in the comfort of the Minshan hotel. Already a day behind schedule, we hope to reach the Fentengxiao reserve that day. The breakfast served in the hostel is a traditional Chinese breakfast, with the addition of a bowl of vicious pickled gherkins and a dry unsweetened sponge cake, thankfully unique to this county.

THERE ARE MANY SMALL STALLS ON THE STREET BELOW OUR WINDOW; THE LOCAL PEOPLE ARE SELLING THEIR SURPLUS GOODS WHICH ARE NOT ALREADY CONTRACTED TO THE STATE. CRATES OF APPLES AND ORANGES, CHILLIES AND PEPPERS, STAND BESIDE CLUSTERS OF SQUAWKING CHICKENS.

Setting out once again, we climb ever higher to the point where the mountain range which forms the edge of the Sichuan basin meets the eastern edge of the plateau borderlands of Tibet. The area is known as the Ganzi Tibetan Autonomous Prefecture, a remote region where the mainly Tibetan and Qiang populations retain some degree of independence. Along with other minority ethnic groups living in China they are exempt from the law restricting each family to one child.

Half an hour's drive from Baoxin town, we catch up with an open-backed army truck filling the narrow track. A group of Chinese soldiers is sprawled in the back, smoking, talking, sleeping. One of them catches sight of Daphne and the whole truck comes to life. We gather that they have not seen women for a long time and the combination of the two of

us and our attractive young interpreter is almost too much for them. As the track widens, and Mr Jing attempts to overtake, they will not allow us to pass. Thus we drive in convoy for several miles, weaving from one side of the road to the other. The soldiers hang out of the back of the truck trying to throw cigarettes through Mr Jing's open window to bribe us to remain behind. Having spent time in the army, he has some sympathy with them and soon engages in a shouted conversation. They are travelling to join the Chinese soldiers already in Tibet for a six-month posting. I am struck by how young they look. The eldest looks around sixteen; it is hard to believe that they are part of the feared Chinese army. We trundle along behind them for a couple of hours, the soldiers grinning like lunatics all the time, until they eventually turn off down another road and with much shouting and waving vanish into the distance. We gradually pick up speed. One way or another the journey is taking far longer than planned.

The roads are still in a dreadful state of repair. Mr Jing negotiates the rough ground skillfully, but our knuckles are turning white as we cling onto the seats in front in sheer terror. The stones and rocks scattered along the track are gradually

THE AREA IS KNOWN AS THE GANZI
TIBETAN AUTONOMOUS
PREFECTURE, A REMOTE REGION
WHERE THE MAINLY TIBETAN AND
QIANG POPULATIONS RETAIN SOME
DEGREE OF INDEPENDENCE.

changing from dull shades of grey and brown to pale and gleaming white chips, until the entire length of the road stretching ahead of us appears to shine white. Looking ahead, we see a huge marble mountain rising out of the landscape, dazzlingly white in the morning sun.

Beyond the Marble Mountain

. . . A HUGE MARBLE MOUNTAIN
RISING OUT OF THE LANDSCAPE.

Approaching, we see that an entire industry has grown up around this natural spectacle. At the base of the mountain the marble is being quarried; huge white rocks are being heaved onto the backs of trucks by manpower alone. There is no mechanical lifting equipment to be seen, just a complex system of logs, ropes and brute strength. The vast boulders are then transferred in their entirety to the marble cutting plants. Vast circular saws slice through the stone, water cascading constantly over the blocks to dampen down the dust. The blocks of marble are cut down further and further into slabs, unless of exceptional quality, when they are kept whole for the carving of statues. This skilled work is also carried out on site, and we drive through rows of statues in various stages of completion. Impressive finished carvings of lions and dragons sit wrapped in plastic sheeting waiting to be transported to their destination – the entrances to temples and important public buildings.

Several hours beyond the marble mountain, jolting and slithering our way along the track, we come to another settlement, the largest we have seen since leaving Baoxin. Daphne stops and, talking to some of the local residents, ascertains that we are in Bao'ergfaijin, and still a good half day's drive from Fentengxiao. It is nearly dusk and we are already tired. The constant shaking and rattling makes the journey twice as tiring as it would otherwise seem. There is a small hostel here, a traditional Zhaodhaisuo providing basic shelter for local travellers. Daphne makes the necessary arrangements to rent rooms for the night but, having seen the reaction to us in Baoxin, leaves us in the truck and omits to mention that we are English until the negotiations are complete. The manager's face is a picture as two dusty and bedraggled blonde aliens eventually emerge from the vehicle and present themselves in the entrance. As we have been driving through Baoxin county we have learnt a new phrase to add to our very slowly expanding Chinese vocabulary. *Lau wai*, meaning foreigners, has been shouted in every town in which we have stopped. The news of *lau wai* spreads like wildfire through this small community and the street is soon crowded with people jostling to catch a glimpse of us. We return to the vehicle to collect our cases

People very friendly & very interested in us. Baby carried in rough cloth sling with broad straps crossing chest.

75

THE DAIRY I KEPT ALONG THE WAY.

FRESH NOODLES HANG OUT TO DRY
IN THE OPEN AIR.

and the crowds part like the Red Sea to let us through. As I bend down to pick up a bag, the crowd leans forward with me, as I straighten up again, they lean back in unison. Rather than heave my large case up to the room, I open it and transfer a few overnight things to a smaller bag. My audience is enthralled. Those closest to me peer over my shoulder at the contents of my case, turning to describe them to those behind whose vision is blocked. With a sudden attack of modesty, I quickly tuck my underwear away under a sweater.

We have a room to ourselves, but there is no private bathroom here, just a central washroom with cold water only and one squat toilet. Despite all the dire warnings before we left, our accommodation has been for the most part very reasonable, if none too clean. We have not been troubled by insects to any great degree. This room is small and plain, the beds are hard wood, but the mattresses covering the base are made of felt, so should prove reasonably soft. The only decoration in the room is provided by a small cracked mirror, hung

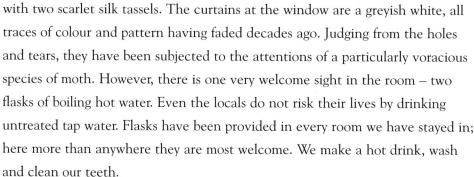

with two scarlet silk tassels. The curtains at the window are a greyish white, all traces of colour and pattern having faded decades ago. Judging from the holes and tears, they have been subjected to the attentions of a particularly voracious species of moth. However, there is one very welcome sight in the room – two flasks of boiling hot water. Even the locals do not risk their lives by drinking untreated tap water. Flasks have been provided in every room we have stayed in; here more than anywhere they are most welcome. We make a hot drink, wash and clean our teeth.

Much refreshed, we join Daphne and Mr Jing and make our way down the main street to find an evening meal. There are three or four eating houses, all open to the street; the food is being cooked on traditional stone ovens to be inspected by passers-by. Daphne peers into the black pots, prods ingredients, sniffs, tastes, consults the cooks. Eventually she makes her selection and we file in. So do the large crowd which has followed our halting progress through the small town. It soon becomes clear that it will be impossible for us to eat at one of the three tables in the small restaurant, and equally difficult to serve any other clients, as our mass of followers are entirely blocking the entrance, the gaps between the tables and most of the street outside.

永

The owner of the restaurant solves this impasse by guiding us through to her private room at the back, where we can use the family's dining table and eat in peace. The crowds are shepherded out of the restaurant and we are left alone, apart from a few children who occasionally dart in and out, giggling and pointing. The room we are in is small and quite dark. As well as being the living- and dining-room for the family who own the restaurant, it also serves as the larder. We eat surrounded by stacks of fresh green vegetables, sacks of rice and bags of tea. On the floor by the table is a bucket containing the meat for the evening's dishes.

A huge quantity of food is placed before us – cooked at the front and brought to the table as soon as it is ready. We eat slices of aubergine with chillies, beans with chillies, chillies with chillies. This is Sichuan cooking at its most typical. A large plate of thin strips of pork, cooked with spring onions and coated in a garlic sauce is served. This is a dish we have had at practically every meal, a staple of the region. It is delicious.

We return to the hostel to find that the water in our flasks has not been replaced; all we have to clean our teeth is half a mug of cold tea.

THE FOOD IS BEING COOKED ON TRADITIONAL STONE OVENS TO BE INSPECTED BY PASSERS-BY.

FISH IN SICHUAN HOT SAUCE

Serves 4

Catch of the day (carp, bream or grey mullet are ideal)
1 tbsp soy sauce
1 tbsp rice wine
Vegetable oil

Sauce
2 cloves garlic (finely chopped)
3 spring onions (finely chopped)
1 tbsp ginger root (finely chopped)
2 tbsp chilli bean sauce
1 tbsp tomato purée
2 tbsp rice vinegar
fi cup of water
1 tbsp cornflour
fi tsp sesame oil

Step 1
Wash the fish. Dry well. Score on both sides with 5 or 6 diagonal cuts to the bone to allow marinade to soak into flesh. Pour soy sauce and wine on both sides, leave to marinate in fridge for at least 15 minutes.

Step 2
Heat the oil in a pre-heated wok until smoking. Deep fry the fish for approximately 4 minutes on both sides or until golden.

Step 3
Pour off the oil, leaving just enough to cover the base of the wok. Move the fish to one side, add all the garlic, the white parts of the spring onions, chilli bean sauce, tomato purée, sugar vinegar and water. Bring to the boil and braise the fish in the sauce for approximately 5 minutes, turning it over once.

Step 4
Add the green parts of the spring onions, and thicken the sauce with cornflour. Sprinkle with sesame oil and serve immediately.

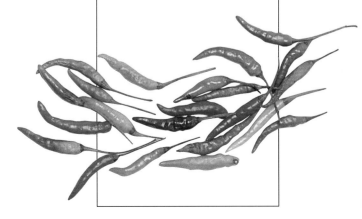

Chapter Ten

W

大熊猫

ILD pandas lead a solitary life in isolated pockets in the mountainside forests of Sichuan, Ganxi and Sha'anxi. Living in ranges of between three and four square kilometres, they rarely come into contact with other members of their species outside the brief breeding season. The range of one individual may overlap to some extent with that of another, but the two pandas will generally avoid one another, leaving a scent-marked trail to advertise their presence and outline their territory. The panda requires a constant supply of bamboo, as well as a source of fresh water; they need to feed for around fourteen hours a day.

Fossil records show that the species was at its most widespread about 1.8 million years ago. Remains indicate that numbers began to decline between 10,000 and 20,000 years ago, roughly around the end of the last ice age. As the earth warmed, pandas retreated to higher altitudes. The lowland plains became more densely forested and less suited to the growth of bamboo, the panda's staple food.

In modern times, numbers have declined sharply. Biological and environmental factors appear to conspire against the survival of the species. Poaching for skins, and accidental trapping in illegal snares set for musk deer, have severely eroded an already small population. Naturally occurring problems such as the occasional die back of bamboo also incur a harsh toll. Disease such as asicariasis (roundworm disease), which is believed to be carried by seventy per cent of all pandas, can affect growth and reproduction even when it is not fatal. They are also vulnerable to other diseases and infections. The major problem, however, would seem to be the extensive cultivation and deforestation of mainland China, which has severely constricted their habitat.

Much of the bamboo forest which once covered China has been destroyed for timber and cleared for farmland. It is estimated that in the past twenty years the panda's territory has been halved. The steady encroachment of agriculture on the landscape has pushed the panda population into an ever smaller area. Pandas find themselves hemmed in on all sides by human settlements, unable to cover wide stretches of agricultural land to alternative food sources should their own fail. Because their bamboo diet is difficult to digest fully, they cannot go for much more than six hours at a time without eating.

The erosion of habitat also results in groups of pandas being cut off from one another in isolated populations causing interbreeding within a limited gene pool. Over several generations this can lead to weaker animals, with less natural resistance to disease and decreased fertility. As we drove ever closer to the panda's mountain home, we were acutely aware that the miles of farmland which sustains China's human population tragically contributes to the continuing decline of China's giant panda population.

TIBETAN FARMHOUSES DECORATED WITH INTRICATE COLOURED PATTERNS.

Recognising the acute need to protect what remains of the country's unspoilt wild areas, the Chinese government established fifty nature reserves as far back as the 1950s. The conservation programme suffered a severe setback during the years of the Cultural Revolution in the 1960s. However, recent co-operation with foreign governments, the United Nations and conservation organisations, including the World Wide Fund for Nature, has resulted in the number of designated reserves being increased to nearly five hundred. Twelve of these reserves are home to the giant panda. Public access to these areas is restricted, and farming and land development strictly limited.

The Fentengxiao Reserve for the Preservation of the Giant Panda was established by the Chinese government in 1975. Separated from the Wolong reserve by a high ridge of mountain peaks, it covers an area of four hundred square kilometres. Smaller and far less accessible than Wolong, it has not attracted the same international attention. It was in this region that Chi-Chi, one of London Zoo's most famous residents, was captured in 1958. Funded in the main by the Chinese government, it receives comparatively little in the way of outside donations, though some money has been sent from the United States and Japan.

THE STEADY ENCROACHMENT OF AGRICULTURE ON THE LANDSCAPE HAS PUSHED THE PANDA INTO AN EVER SMALLER AREA.

Our intended destination was a small hospital for sick pandas, also built in 1975, which is located deep within the reserve.

Day Twelve

7.00 am. I am in bed. Pollyanna has ventured out to the washroom. I am just contemplating getting dressed when the door is flung open. The manageress stalks in, her face set in stone. She strides past the end of my bed, removes the flasks, turns and marches out again, slamming the door behind her. Not a glance, not a greeting. I wonder if there is anywhere more private to dress.

A typical Chinese breakfast sets us up for the day. I am developing a taste for the steamed bread, but the cold pickled spring onions still leave me without the power of speech this early in the morning.

We set out, following the Ching Yee, a tributary of the Min river. The tracks here are heavily used by logging trucks, and are prone to disintegration from land slides. In places the going is very muddy and slippery; we slide and slither along, and at times sink deep into the mud, but never quite grinding to a complete halt. We have been driving now for three days and I am starting to feel distinctly shaken up and saddle sore, but now Fentengxiao is just a few hours drive ahead of us. However, we are to make one final diversion before we reach our intended destination.

FARMERS ATTEMPTING TO PLOUGH THE STONE-COVERED GROUND.

Instead of driving directly to the border of the Fentengxiao reserve, we make a very slight detour, to the peak of one of the honey pot mountains. Perched high on the summit is a Buddhist temple, reputedly the most beautiful in the region. We climb rapidly, despite the fact that the track is only just wide enough to accommodate the truck. Thankfully we do not meet any other traffic. The road here is barely completed. Teams of women are working at the roadside, digging deep trenches and lifting huge piles of stones and bricks. In places there is no road at all, and we crawl more slowly and uncertainly over landslips and scree. We climb higher and higher, heading towards the Tibetan settlement below the temple. The agriculture on the mountain slopes is quite different here. The crops are planted in larger fields, stretching up the mountainsides. We pass farmers attempting to plough the stone-covered ground with oxen; the soil looks grey, barren and rocky and they would seem to have set themselves a Herculean task. We pass a few farm houses, quite different in appearance from those in the Chinese villages; these are two-storey

PERCHED HIGH ON THE SUMMIT IS A BUDDHIST TEMPLE.

THE WONDERFULLY ORNATE TEMPLE.

constructions, the lower rooms built of grey stone, the upper levels of timber. Many have balconies that are beautifully decorated with intricate coloured patterns.

We pass through the village towards the temple, clearly visible ahead of us on top of the mountain, with golden roof tiles gleaming brightly in the strong sunlight. There is a sheer drop on one side of the track; Mr Jing hugs the truck to the wall of the mountain. A series of hairpin bends carries us steadily upwards, until the temple appears to be no longer in front, but way behind us, and we feel that we are driving further and further away from it. We must have taken the wrong road from the village. There only seemed to be one track, but the temple is receding like a mirage. A decision is made. We will head back to the village and start again on another road. This means that Mr Jing must make a three-point turn to take us back the way we have travelled. In the event this is more like a thirty-three point turn, Mr Jing heaving the wheel round, mumbling under his breath, as the front wheels touch the edge of the overhang and small stones bounce away down the sheer mountainside. I may never recover from the experience. Nor, I suspect, will Mr Jing, who looked in desperate need of a lie down in a cool dark room by the end of the manoeuvre. We head slowly back towards the village, until Daphne spots a group of women working in one of the fields and gets out to ask directions. Although we are too far away to hear any of the conversation, it soon becomes evident from the pointing that we were in fact heading in the right direction to begin with. Mr Jing chokes on his mouthful of water and sprays it out of the car window. We drive back to the village to turn round again, before heading once more towards the temple.

The effort was worthwhile. The temple is spectacular. There is a small shrine at one end of a large open courtyard. Intricately painted signs above the doorway are lettered in both Chinese and Tibetan characters. The doors are open and we peer into the dark interior. There are gilt statues, golden urns, sticks of smouldering incense and ornately gilded fabrics. Low walls stretch around the courtyard, the orange tiles above them supported by white pillars. The roofs all curve upwards at the edges, to prevent the entry of ghosts and demons into holy ground – according to local superstition these unwanted spirits can only travel in straight lines.

At either end of the main yard, flights of steps lead to other levels, behind the altar we walk up to other smaller courtyards. At the opposite end the steps lead down the mountainside

Interior of temple very
"happening" – lots of colour –
mainly red & gold – lots of pattern
& carving / dark / heady scent
of incense

Many carvings & statues
of the Buddha

to small plateaux; on each stands a small open pagoda topped with the same golden tiles glowing warmly in the sun. Daphne greets the temple workers. I sit on the wall of one of the higher courtyards and look out at the spectacular views, framed by the white pillars and gleaming roofs. Ridges of blue-grey mountains stretch away into the distance. It is a beautiful day, the sun in shining more strongly than at any time since our arrival in China; even at the top of the mountain it is gloriously warm. Unusually there is hardly any mist clinging to the slopes. The sky is clear and blue, red kites soar high above the mountain peaks, gliding and wheeling on the thermals, sometimes silhouetted against the bright sky, then sunlit against the soft green background of the mountains. Looking out from the temple, I can see clearly why Sichuan, the most lushly green and fertile province of China, has been described through the centuries as Heaven on Earth.

THERE ARE GILT STATUES, GOLDEN URNS, STICKS OF SMOULDERING INCENSE AND ORNATELY GILDED FABRICS.

I am starting to feel at peace with myself, the universe and all within it, when suddenly the air of tranquillity is shattered. I nearly fall off the wall in shock. We have noticed as we have travelled that the Chinese as a race appear to abhor silence the way nature abhors a vacuum, and wherever possible will fill it with sound – music, singing, conversation, usually as loud as possible.

SPECTACULAR VIEWS FRAMED BY WHITE PILLARS AND GOLDEN ROOFS.

<small>FIRST TIME IN FRONT OF THE CAMERA FOR THIS VENERABLE TIBETAN MONK.</small>

This trend has obviously reached even these remote Tibetan settlements, for a teeth-grating wail suddenly blasts out from what must be one of the oldest loud speakers in existence. The initial notes die away and through the crackling and hissing we are able to identify the strains of traditional Tibetan music. This should have proved wonderfully atmospheric, adding to the ambience of the temple like the soundtrack of a film, but unfortunately I cannot shake my conviction that the tape is playing at slightly the wrong speed.

My reverie broken, I make my way down to the courtyard where Pollyanna has been introduced to the only permanent resident of the temple, an elderly Buddhist monk, dressed in purple and saffron robes. We would like to take a photograph of him in the temple so, in order to ask his permission, form ourselves into a bizarre interpreting chain. We ask Daphne in English, she appeals on our behalf to one of the temple workers in Chinese, he translates our request in Tibetan and yells it into the priest's ear, who we learn is eighty-three and somewhat deaf. Some considerable time, and much discussion later, a reply comes back to us. It emerges that the monk has never had his photograph taken before. However, he would be pleased for us to take a picture, on condition that we send him a copy. Naturally we promise to do so. We are lead to the edge of the courtyard. With some ceremony, the monk sits on a low stone chair and motions for

BUDDHISM

Historically, China has always been tolerant of all religious beliefs. Despite ideological differences, those of differing religions have co-existed side by side in relative peace, without threat of persecution. Most Chinese people follow one of the 'Three Ways' – Taosim, Confucianism or Buddhism, the latter being the most widespread religion. Small groups of Muslims and Christians can also be found. Under Communist rule, however, all religious practice was discouraged as being contradictory to the ideals of Communism.

Buddhism came to China from India in the 1st century AD. Buddhists follow the teachings of the Buddha, Siddhartha Gautama, a north Indian prince born *circa* 563 BC. He devoted his life to the search for personal peace, or enlightenment. A respected teacher, he encouraged people to look at the results of their thoughts and actions; he also advocated the search for the blissful state of Nirvana through meditation and the renunciation of worldly desires. Those who attain Nirvana find peace from the sorrows of the world, and break the endless cycle of reincarnation – the prevailing Indian belief at that time. The word Buddha means the enlightened one. Buddhists believe that there have been many buddhas through history and that there are more yet to come.

After the death of the Buddha two main schools of Buddhism developed – Theravada and Mahayana. Despite some differing principles, the two groups co-exist in harmony and friendship. Buddhist teachers from Nepal and China introduced the Mahayanan belief to Tibet and the borderlands in the 7th century – and it became the country's principle religion. The first monastery was built in Tibet in 775 AD.

The Tibetans began to develop their own individual form of Buddhism, with monks called Lamas, which translates loosely as teachers. The Dalai Lama is both their spiritual leader and the ruler of Tibet. The current Dalai Lama fled Tibet in 1959, along with around 100,000 other refugees nine years after the invasion by Communist China. Under Chinese rule, many Buddhist temples and monasteries have been destroyed. Still in exile from his homeland, the Dalai Lama travels the world drawing attention to the plight of Tibet.

TAOISM

Taoists are followers of the teachings of Lao-tzu, known as the old philosopher he was born *circa* 604 BC. He wrote a text called the *Taoerdejing*, which laid out his belief that people should live in harmony with nature.

Taoists believe that it is possible to discover the elixir of life, and become immortal. They worship a group of eight figures, the 'xian' – immortals each possessed of a supernatural power, including the ability to turn objects into gold, raise the dead and become invisible at will.

CONFUCIANISM

Confucianism has shaped the thoughts of the Chinese people over several millennia. During his lifetime (551 - 479 BC) Confucius developed a moral outlook based on kindness, respect for others and traditional family life. Believing that strong families were the basis of a stable society, he encouraged ancestor worship, leading the Chinese to view themselves as part of a long line of family members, including those long dead, and those yet to be born. He was opposed to slavery in all forms, but believed in obedience to a fair master. The basis of his philosophy can be summed up in the phrase, 'Let the Prince be a Prince, the Minister a Minister, the Father a Father, and the Son a Son'.

Traditional head-dress for mother and child!

The seamstress from the village.

All of the women are wearing traditional national costume: a long black cloak, called a chuba, belted at the waist over an ankle-length skirt, and beautiful head-dresses of twisted black cloth, wound into the plaits of their hair and decorated with silver, turquoise and amber.

us to kneel beside him. We pass the camera to Daphne and she takes a photograph of this strange group of three. As soon as the photography is complete, he rises, bows slightly and returns to the temple buildings.

Driving back, we stop in the main, indeed the only, street running through the Tibetan village. We walk down the road between the timbered buildings. A complete silence falls in the village as we progress. Mothers dart into the street and whisk their children back into the safety of buildings, old women wave garlic at us from the shelter of doorways. We attempt to look benign and eventually, with Daphne's help, make some contact and are able to take a few photographs. All of the women are wearing traditional national costume: a long black cloak, called a chuba, belted at the waist over an ankle-length skirt, and beautiful head-dresses of twisted black cloth, wound into the plaits of their hair and decorated with silver, turquoise and amber. Even the women working in the fields and on the roads are wearing the full traditional clothing. Here, more than anywhere, we encountered wariness rather than curiosity. None of the people Daphne spoke to had seen a Westerner before; for the two of us suddenly to appear in the middle of the high street must have come as quite a shock for the local population.

Leaving the stunned village behind us, we drive back down to the main road and turn off towards Fentengxiao. The final part of the journey seems remarkably quick. In just under two hours we have reached the border of a place which I had started to believe only existed in books.

Now, however, we find ourselves finally facing the red and white barrier stretching across the road, marking the edge of the protected area. Two officials walk over to the car and we show them our relevant passes and documents, some of them obtained in England prior to our departure, others collected from the government offices in Chengdu. The guards study them, then study us. They walk away a little distance, there is much muttering. They return to the car. No, they are sorry, they cannot admit us into the reserve.

We are horrified. Are our passes not in order? Yes, they seem to be, but they have not been given instructions to allow Westerners into the reserve. We can see the hospital building just a few hundred metres from the

WE ARE STILL THERE AN HOUR AND A HALF LATER. AFTER MUCH HAGGLING AND NEGOTIATION A COMPROMISE HAS BEEN REACHED. THEY WILL RAISE THE BARRIER. WE CAN GO TO THE HOSPITAL AND INTRODUCE OURSELVES, AND STAY FOR ONE HOUR.

barrier. It is agonising to have driven so far, only to be turned away at this point, with seemingly no other option than to head straight back to Chengdu.

We were, however, forgetting Daphne. Having travelled with us for quite some time, she has come to regard us as friends, rather than just employers. All that she has to do, to fulfil her job description, is interpret anything we ask, and help us with the booking of accommodation. However, she is equally distressed at being turned away after four days of travelling and launches into a heated debate with the guards. She goes back over our documentation, she tells them how far we have travelled, that we have come from England just to visit this hospital. She describes Pollyanna's work as an artist, talks of our love of animals. We are frustrated, sitting tensely in the back of the vehicle, while the heated discussion rages in quick fire Chinese. We can only watch as Daphne argues on our behalf, hands waving in our direction.

We are still there an hour and a half later. After much haggling and negotiation a compromise has been reached. They will raise the barrier. We can go to the hospital and introduce ourselves, and stay for one hour. We can take one photograph only, and on no account can we use a video camera.

POLLYANNA AND ANNA-LOUISE WITH YANG BEN QING.

The barrier is lifted. We drive through and park at the hospital entrance. There we are met by the director of the nature reserve and hospital, Yang Ben Qing. He shakes our hands and smiles, but seems wary of us. Conscious of our limited time, we ask if we can be shown round the hospital. We are led down the drive through a passage to an open yard. On three sides there are buildings – pens for the injured animals and the workers' living quarters. In the centre is a flower bed surrounded by a low wall, a few shrubs poking through the overgrown plants. The fourth side opens out into a natural paddock surrounded by a high concrete wall.

There are currently three giant pandas receiving treatment in the hospital. We are led to the first of the pens and shown a three-year-old male with a damaged ear. The wound was turning septic when he was brought in, but he has been treated and is now recovering well. Mr Qing expects him to be returned to the wild within the week. The second panda we are shown was picked up when it was very weak, on the edge of starvation, apparently suffering from digestive problems. Again it has responded well to treatment and is now eating almost normally. The third

INSIDE THE PEN WITH THE YOUNG
PANDA WITH THE INJURED EAR.

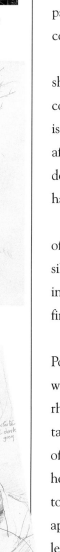

panda, on the other hand, looks very sick indeed. Brought in only days earlier, she is suffering from pneumonia and is lying on one side, barely moving. We can hear the breath rattling in her chest and she is coughing almost continually. When we quietly approach she does not raise her head, barely moving her eyes to look at us. Even her fur seems matted and discoloured, the white patches a dull yellow. They have started to treat the illness, but Mr Qing is obviously still very concerned about her condition.

All the time we are walking round, Daphne is beside us, talking non-stop to Mr Qing, whom she recognises as possessing the ultimate authority at the hospital. She is constantly trying to convince him to let us stay for longer than the hour allotted to us by the guards at the gate. She is wonderful. She puts our case forward as best she can, asking for permission to stay the whole afternoon, to take more than one photograph, to allow Pollyanna to make some sketches. She describes our previous working trips to India, Africa and the Arctic, talks about the animals we have studied, about the British wildlife we have cared for in England, about Pollyanna's painting.

Mr Qing begins to take an interest in us, and to ask us some questions. Daphne has the idea of fetching Pollyanna's sketch pad. He leafs through the sketches of the pandas at Wolong in silence, then turns to Pollyanna and beckons. We all follow. We pass through a low wooden door into a small concrete yard, then through a small metal door. I step through, straighten up, and find myself face to face with a panda.

We are inside the pen with the young panda with the injured ear. Mr Qing would like Pollyanna to make a sketch of the bear. A small stool is brought in for Pollyanna, and she starts work. Fresh bamboo is brought for the panda to chew on; he sits opposite us, munching rhythmically, but watching us all the time. I take my one photograph. Mr Qing motions that I can take more. He stands looking over Pollyanna's shoulder, occasionally commenting on the progress of the work. Relations seem to be improving. I glance surreptitiously at my watch, we have been here nearly an hour and a half already. Some milk is brought in for the panda to drink, he stands to lap from the metal bowl. After finishing the milk, he advances towards us, pauses, then approaches again. Mr Qing flaps his hands urgently towards the door, and we rise quickly and leave. The panda paces up and down a couple of times, then settles down again to his meal of bamboo. Although pandas appear to be the friendliest of animals, with their flat faces and

appealing expressions, they can, like any large wild animal, be very dangerous. Originally pandas hunted for food, and they are still classified as carnivores. They have five long sharp claws on each large paw and are capable of doing a great deal of damage with one careless swipe.

When the bear has settled again and is once more chewing steadily on the fresh leaves and shoots, we are allowed back in the pen. After a further half an hour we leave, and Mr Qing shows us round the other residents of the hospital. There are two pens of red pandas, two in each, scurrying up to the higher platforms as we approach, then peering cautiously at us over the edge. Next to them is a cage filled with six monkeys. Constantly chattering and leaping, they reach through the wire to try and grab our clothes and pull at our camera straps. Beside them is a large aviary housing a wide variety of exotically coloured pheasants. By now dusk is falling and our time limit appears to have been abandoned. Mr Qing has thawed measurably towards us since our arrival; through Daphne he invites us to stay for dinner. We are delighted to accept.

ORIGINALLY PANDAS HUNTED FOR FOOD, AND THEY ARE STILL CLASSIFIED AS CARNIVORES. THEY HAVE FIVE LONG SHARP CLAWS ON EACH LARGE PAW AND ARE CAPABLE OF DOING A GREAT DEAL OF DAMAGE WITH ONE CARELESS SWIPE.

So, a short while later, we find ourselves sitting round a low wooden table with Daphne, Mr Jing, Mr Qing and four other men who work full time in the hospital. The food is prepared, cooked and eaten in a communal dining area, which is in fact the corner of one of the worker's bedrooms. Everyone pitches in to help with the cooking, except for us – we are excused, having failed the basic test of being able to identify most of the ingredients. A wide variety of dishes is prepared in a single iron cooking dish over an open stove: bamboo shoots in a light sauce; shredded fried potato (the first I have eaten since reaching China); pork and spring onions; cabbage and the shoots of wild plants; a 'soup' made from lettuce and haricot beans. The food prepared here is less spicy than any we have been offered previously, though the ubiquitous chillies are still very much in evidence.

MR QING WOULD LIKE POLLYANNA TO MAKE A SKETCH OF THE BEAR.

By now we are getting on remarkably well with Mr Qing and all of the workers. Even though the conversation is very long winded, with poor Daphne having to translate everything two ways, there is much laughter. We entertain everyone simply by being blonde, and by demonstrating our unique technique with chopsticks.

A WIDE VARIETY OF DISHES IS PREPARED IN A SINGLE IRON COOKING DISH OVER AN OPEN STOVE.

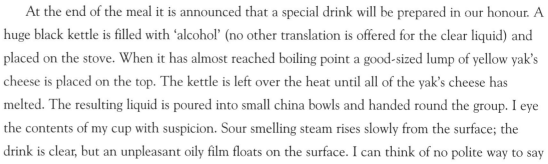

EVERYONE PITCHES IN TO HELP WITH THE COOKING, EXCEPT FOR US – WE ARE EXCUSED, HAVING FAILED THE BASIC TEST OF BEING ABLE TO IDENTIFY MOST OF THE INGREDIENTS.

At the end of the meal it is announced that a special drink will be prepared in our honour. A huge black kettle is filled with 'alcohol' (no other translation is offered for the clear liquid) and placed on the stove. When it has almost reached boiling point a good-sized lump of yellow yak's cheese is placed on the top. The kettle is left over the heat until all of the yak's cheese has melted. The resulting liquid is poured into small china bowls and handed round the group. I eye the contents of my cup with suspicion. Sour smelling steam rises slowly from the surface; the drink is clear, but an unpleasant oily film floats on the surface. I can think of no polite way to say that I have given up drinking molten yak's cheese, so I close my eyes, think of England, and take a cautious sip.

It tastes like hot Scotch whisky, multiplied to the power of ten, with a dash of slightly sour cream. It burns down my throat and warms my stomach with a red glow. It is delicious. I have another mouthful. It still tastes delicious. I have another cup.

Several cups later, it is announced that we cannot possibly drive anywhere now, we must stay the night. We gratefully accept the offer. Mr Jing has entered enthusiastically into a drinking competition with one of the workers, and I suspect that he is in no fit state to negotiate the twists and turns of the narrow roads leading back to the hostel. We are told that we can use the room of one of the men who is currently away working on the mountainside. Mr Qing shows us upstairs to the room himself.

The accommodation is sparse. There are two wooden beds with straw mattresses and woollen blankets, and a table and chair. We are given flasks of hot water. Directly outside our room is a cold water tap above a tiled trough – the washing facilities for the entire hospital. At the far end of the corridor, past all the other rooms, a door leads out onto a balcony. Going back off the balcony there are two more rooms. The first houses a squat toilet. I glance in the second room, it is much larger, and open to the balcony, but appears to be empty. I am on the verge of leaving when I spot a small metal tank in the far corner, high up on the wall, with a tap sticking out of it. I have found the shower.

I return to the bedroom, to prepare for the night. It has been a highly eventful day, and it is now very late. I am extremely tired. A long drive, a morning spent in the temple, a tense scene at the barrier, a wonderful afternoon with the pandas and too much alcohol and yak's cheese have combined to bring on exhaustion. I am ready to collapse on the mattress and sleep for several hours.

There is a knock at the door. One of the workers enters, accompanied by the long-suffering Daphne. We are now the honoured guests of the hospital and they will heat water for us so that we can shower before we go to bed. The shower, unlike the one at Wolong, does not plug in, but needs to be filled with pre-heated water. They will put a barrel over the stove; it will only take about an hour to prepare enough water to fill the tank. I protest weakly, doubting my ability to stay awake for that length of time, and having seen the floor of the shower room.

A typical 'Don't go to any trouble', 'Its no trouble', 'No, no, really' conversation ensues. We compromise. Instead of heating a barrel of water for one of us, we will use half a barrel each for a quick shower. This, we hope, will enable the second person to be in bed before 3.00 am.

An hour passes. The water is heated. I am shaken awake. Pollyanna decides to brave the tap first. I sit and wait, bleary eyed. I am even less keen now that I have discovered that the faint smell of panda which has been following me all evening is in fact coming from my jacket, so unless I shower fully dressed the aroma will remain to haunt me the following morning. Another convincing reason for showering clothed is the night-time temperature. We are 1,500 metres above sea level and it is extremely cold. A third reason, of course, is that the shower room does not possess a door.

Pollyanna returns. I gather my courage and set off to make use of the remaining half tank of water. I return to the room some ten minutes later feeling refreshed and clean. The floor of the shower room, however, was as filthy and slimy as it seemed on my first brief inspection. So, although I finally undress, I keep my boots on.

Anna-lou Takes a shower at FenTenxiou

WITH approximately one thousand pandas remaining in the world, a baby panda is a rare and precious creature.

Baby pandas are tiny at birth, just fifteen centimetres long, weighing only one hundred grams. The babies are hairless, blind and completely helpless. They bury deep in the mother's fur – zoos have been known to miss the birth! They have a surprisingly loud call from the very start – probably, in part, to alert the mother panda to their whereabouts, and prevent her from inadvertently squashing her tiny charge. Female pandas are gentle and devoted mothers, seemingly aware of the vulnerability of their minute cubs. They cradle their cubs in their giant paws, comforting them with little pats, and frequently tenderly licking and nuzzling the tiny babies.

A week after birth the black markings of the eye patches and shoulders are visible on the cub's skin. By the third week the baby looks very much like a miniature adult and can raise its head and crawl. The eyes open fully at one and a half months. Teething begins at around three months, though they continue to suckle the mother's milk until they around six months old. At five months the baby can walk, trot and is beginning to climb. Pandas have a long 'childhood', remaining with the mother until they are eighteen months old, when they gradually become more independent.

Female pandas occasionally give birth to twins, but are unlikely to rear both cubs, usually abandoning one in the first few days.

In his book *The Last Panda*, the American naturalist George Schaller, who has spent his life surrounded by different animals, describes two baby pandas as 'the most endearing creatures I have ever seen'.

Day Thirteen

Daphne arrives in our room at 7.30 am. She has already been up for an hour talking to Mr Qing, and she has some exciting news. We have been invited to stay on at the hospital for a few days. There is, however, one condition. If we stay, we must help out in the hospital. We could not be

永

THE HOSPITAL WORKER WITH A PLUMP, SQUIRMING, BABY PANDA BEAR.

POLLYANNA'S TURN TO ENJOY THE EXPERIENCE.

HE REJOICES IN THE NAME OF 'YIAO YUAN', WHICH WE ARE TOLD TRANSLATES AS TIBETAN HOSPITAL

more thrilled – the prospect of actually working with the pandas is more than we could have ever hoped for, and we eagerly accept the invitation.

At breakfast I cannot face the wok-fried eggs after last night's excesses, but sip delicately at a bowl of warmed yak's milk. After eating, we are led down into the courtyard of the clinic. One of the workers disappears into a small building and reappears a couple of moments later. We can hardly believe our eyes. My mouth opens and closes soundlessly, as if I have just eaten an entire bowl of pepper-fried chillies in garlic. The hospital worker is carrying a plump, squirming baby panda bear.

We had no idea that the hospital was housing a baby as well as the adult pandas we had seen on our arrival. Evidently, during the course of the previous night's meal, we had earned enough trust to be introduced to the hospital's youngest resident. We learn that he is six months old, and has been reared at the clinic from just a few days old.

The cub was found on the mountainside by one of the workers who heard his cry; he searched through the undergrowth until he located the tiny pink cub and then brought him back to the hospital. This is invariably a difficult decision for the workers at Wolong. Female pandas have been known to 'abandon' their cubs on the mountainside for up to fifty hours at a time. Initially he was cared for by Mr Qing, who kept him close at all times, nestled inside his sweater. He fed him almost constantly with drops of milk, and even took him into his own bed at night. Now well past the danger stage, the baby is evidently in excellent health and is full of energy and curiosity. He rejoices in the name of 'Yiao Yuan', which we are told translates as Tibetan hospital. This rather unromantic, but logical, name derives from the fact that he was found on the borders of Tibet and then brought back to the panda hospital.

Pandas do not need to learn to hunt, and can be taught to forage for bamboo. They lead largely solitary lives, so there is little need to worry about their interaction with others of their own species. As Yiao gets older, we are told, he will spend more time with the adult pandas in the hospital. The only worry is that he may never successfully mate, having spent too much formative time with humans to learn the correct panda rituals. However, under the current circumstances many wild pandas can live their entire natural lives in the forests without mating. At least baby

永

Yiao will be able to live an entirely free and natural life on the mountainside once he is old enough to be independent.

It is essential that Yiao learns as much as possible about his forest surroundings from a very early age. He must learn to climb trees and eat bamboo, just as his mother would have taught him. Therefore, each day, he is brought out into the grounds of the hospital to spend as much time as possible outdoors. As he is still very young, he is somewhat lacking in judgement and co-ordination. It is essential that he has constant supervision to prevent him from injuring himself. This is to be our job.

It seems unbelievable. This is not work, it is a privilege beyond our wildest dreams to be given temporary charge of a national treasure. On a practical level, we can see that giving us this employment allows the other workers to perform other essential tasks in the hospital.

Yiao is handed over to Pollyanna. To the delight of the assembled workers he promptly climbs onto her shoulder and tries to eat her hair. We are given his feeding and rest times and then sent out into the natural paddock where he can climb and explore to his heart's content.

Mr Qing tells me that we are at liberty to take photographs and make sketches. I am, however, still not allowed to use my video camera, which remains locked in the truck. It is local government policy to forbid any filming in the region, a law which extends to Chinese film crews as well as foreign visitors.

Pollyanna collects her sketching equipment and the three of us head out for the day. We place Yiao gently on the ground and he is off immediately – rummaging around in the undergrowth, climbing rocks, playing and exploring.

This has to be the ideal opportunity for Pollyanna to complete some drawings. She sits on the ground and I gather up the baby and place him a couple of metres away. Now she can complete her study. Yiao, however, has other ideas. Innately curious, he runs to Pollyanna's feet and tries to eat her hiking boots. Advancing up her legs, he spies the sketch pad and clambers up for a closer look. After inspecting her initial drawings, he starts chewing the pad. This is one art critic with teeth. He chews her pencil, her hair, her right hand. In the end it

THIS IS ONE ART CRITIC WITH TEETH. HE CHEWS HER PENCIL, HER HAIR, HER RIGHT HAND.

WE GIVE HIM A BOTTLE OF MILK
EVERY FEW HOURS.

ARTISTIC ENDEAVOUR IS SOON
ABANDONED IN FAVOUR OF SOME
SERIOUS PLAY.

is easier to abandon any artistic endeavours and play with him instead. Left to his own devices, Yiao is not still for a second. If we turn away for a moment he will have climbed over a rock, disappeared behind bushes, or made an attempt to climb a tree. This is one activity which is to be encouraged – adult giant pandas spend a considerable amount of time in trees and it is essential that he learns this skill.

We are very aware that this little baby is not only the much loved pride and joy of the hospital, but also a designated national treasure. In theory, if he comes to any harm while in our care, we could find ourselves facing a court with the power to impose the death penalty. This particular little treasure seems to have little or no idea which trees are suitable for climbing and which branches will support his weight. We stand below him, barely breathing, as he inches out on ever more precarious twigs, poised to catch him if he should lose his grip and fall. He has a knack for finding trouble, even in the security of the hospital grounds. Climbing over one ridge of rock, he manages to find the hospital's temporary rubbish dump and we have quickly to whisk him to safety out of the reach of broken glass and sharp tins.

Although his teeth are starting to come through, and he is keen to try them out, Yiao is not yet eating solid food. We give him a bottle of milk every few hours. He drinks a special mix of yak's milk, honey and vitamins. An enthusiastic but messy eater, we need a face cloth to clean him up after each feed. Hopefully most of the milk is ending up inside the panda each time, though a good quantity seems to escape onto his fur and our clothes. He lies in our arms to be fed, feet in the air, reaching greedily for the bottle. His fur is thick and coarse, his small black eyes shine brightly, exhibiting a keen interest in his surroundings. Each time he has finished a bottle of milk he reaches out for more, making heartbreaking mewling cries. This is merely a healthy greediness – he is clearly well fed. Dense and compact, he is heavy for his size and, although we fuss over him as if he were made of Dresden china, he is undoubtedly healthy and robust.

After lunch, it is time for his nap. He is returned to his room in the hospital buildings. Over excited and full of energy, he is not ready to sleep. We ask for advice and are told that in order to persuade him that it is time for a nap, we should lie down on the floor ourselves and pretend to doze. Thus we curl up on the straw and close our eyes. Yiao clambers over us, but we try to ignore him and, in time, he also settles down and is soon fast asleep. We creep out quietly. The

worker who usually has charge of Yiao tells us that sometimes, when he is tired himself, he will fall asleep and wake up a couple of hours later to find the baby curled up asleep on his chest.

PANDEMONIUM
Mr R H Cooke (UK).

Chapter Twelve

A 大熊猫

T the outset, our plans for travelling within China were fairly flexible. We had only made definite arrangements to visit Wolong and Fentengxiao. As we had already experienced, it can be hard to predict accurately the length of journey times when travelling in the more remote regions of the countryside. Therefore, although we had details of a couple of other natural reserves, we had not made any fixed plans to move on, preferring to wait and see what happened during our travels.

We decided to accept the kind hospitality offered to us by Mr Qing and remain at Fentengxiao as long as we could. After all, where else would we be offered the once in a lifetime opportunity of having such close contact with a baby panda, or be allowed inside enclosures with wild adult pandas? We also realised that we would be lucky to find such kind and welcoming hosts.

During the next few days we settle into a routine. Rising early, we breakfast with the other workers, spend the day caring for Yiao and retire to bed early.

Yiao is at an age to be gradually weaned from the bottle. The first stage of this process involves teaching him to lap his milk from a shallow tin bowl. Over the course of two or three days, small amounts of crumbled bread and vitamin mix are added to the milk; we also give him sticks of fresh bamboo to chew. Although he gnaws at them enthusiastically, and succeeds in expertly shredding the leaves and shoots, no greenery is reaching his stomach yet. He will not begin to eat solid food regularly until he is nearly a year old.

Pandas are remarkable animals in that they exist on a nutritional knife-edge. Shown by fossil records and anatomical studies to have originally been carnivores, they have, over the centuries, turned to a diet consisting almost exclusively of bamboo. Some recent reports from China have indicated that isolated pockets of pandas may have retained some of their hunting skills; given the opportunity most will scavenge for meat left on the forest floor. Their habit of licking out cooking pots in mountain villages gave rise in past times to the myth that these unusual looking creatures fed on a diet of iron!

永

永

WE TEACH HIM TO LAP HIS MILK
FROM A SHALLOW TIN BOWL

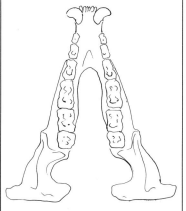

. . . HIS JAW WILL BE POWERFUL
ENOUGH TO CRUSH THE STRONG
BAMBOO STEMS.

For the majority of pandas, however, a typical day's diet will consist of twelve to fifteen kilograms of bamboo. The panda is unable to digest efficiently the specialist diet to which it restricts itself because it retains the simple digestive tract of a carnivore. Bamboo is a poor source of energy for a panda and yet they consume the leaves and stems indiscriminately, barely chewing as they eat. George Schaller's extensive studies at Wolong led him to suggest that a panda only assimilates nutrients from approximately seventeen per cent of the food it eats. A herbivore, like a deer, will assimilate eighty per cent of the food it eats. A carnivore, such as a lion, digests with an efficiency of up to ninety per cent. Pandas are effectively only hours away from starvation at any time; they must eat constantly to gain sufficient energy to survive on their low-quality diet. It is a mystery why this baby, like the rest of his species, attempts to exist on a diet which on the surface appears entirely unsuitable. Although pandas are capable of eating alternative foods, they have often been observed ignoring nutritious fruits and berries while making straight for a clump of bamboo. It appears that for most pandas bamboo equals food. Nothing else counts.

Bamboo does have one big advantage as a food source – it is available all the year round. A panda living on this diet would not be able to eat enough surplus food to acquire a thick layer of fat to enable them to hibernate through the cold winter months, so they continue to feed throughout the year on the lush green shoots which show no seasonal alteration.

Like all pandas, Yiao has some adaptations which will help him to feed efficiently on his chosen diet. His teeth will grow large and flat, his jaw will be powerful enough to crush the strong bamboo stems. He already possesses a modified wrist bone, supple enough to use like an opposable thumb, enabling him to grip and manipulate his food with ease.

At such a young age, Yiao still requires regular rest and during his nap times Pollyanna takes the opportunity to sketch the other residents of the hospital. She is allowed in the pens with the adult pandas on several more occasions, sketching for hours at a time. The workers take quite an interest in her drawings, wandering over at intervals to cast a critical eye over her work, and pointing out any inaccuracies. As few people in the world can be more familiar with pandas, Pollyanna is delighted when their expressions are favourable and the sounds and smiles appear to be complimentary. Nobody in the hospital speaks English, and though we still have Daphne to translate for us, she is spending a great deal of time in her room at the hospital, conscientiously

永

AN ENTHUSIASTIC BUT MESSY EATER.

writing her account of the journey for her employers. Mr Jing is tending to the truck, checking that it has survived the rough and ready tracks intact. He also cleans it until it is gleaming – as soon as we drive away from the hospital gates it will be coated once more in mud and dust, but for the time being it is polished and shiny.

Pollyanna also sits in the pens with the red pandas to add to the sketches she made at Wolong. She takes the opportunity to sit in the aviary to sketch the motley assortment of pheasants.

Mr Qing continues to be a generous and considerate host. He is delighted at our interest in China's natural history. On one occasion he takes us to the boundaries of the hospital to show us another of his rare and valuable natural treasures. This time it is a plant, a small tree, standing around a metre high. We are told that it is one of forty species under special government protection. Daphne translates its name for us as 'pigeon tree' but, looking in our reference books later that day, I discover that it is *Davidia involuorata*, the dove tree. Its romantic local name comes from the white flowers which it will bear later in the year – when the wind blows the long white petals flutter like the wings of doves resting in the branches. Initially catalogued by Père David, and still carrying his name, the dove tree remains unchanged since prehistoric times, providing naturalists with an invaluable living link to China's earliest natural history. Surviving plants like these provide our best clues to the ecological environment existing before the last ice age, a time when pandas could still be found throughout the country.

DAVIDIA INVOLUORATA, THE DOVE TREE - WHEN THE WIND BLOWS THE LONG
WHITE PETALS FLUTTER LIKE THE WINGS OF DOVES RESTING IN THE BRANCHES.

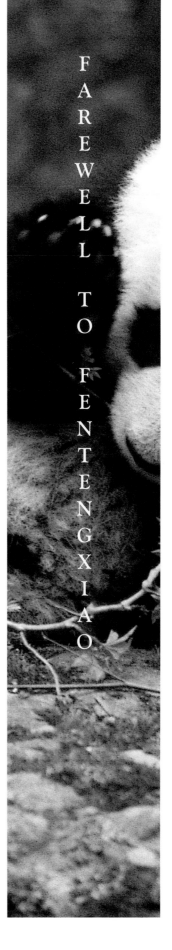

Chapter Thirteen

大熊猫

Throughout our stay at Fentengxiao we are incredibly impressed by the dedication of all the staff at the hospital. Mr Qing is assisted at the clinic by six full-time workers who live at the hospital. An older Tibetan man also lives on site, performing odd jobs and general manual work. The workers live in spartan conditions, and are paid just three hundred yuan a month. By contrast, it costs four hundred yuan a day to feed and care for baby Yiao. Working long hours, apparently without tiring, the genuine love of these men for the pandas in their care shines through. The baby in particular is adored; every possible effort is made to give him a natural and healthy start in life.

During our time at Fentengxiao only four of the six full-time workers were in residence at the hospital. The policy in the reserve is for two of the men to head out at regular intervals to cover the four hundred square kilometres of mountainside in the reserve. Camping out at night for a fortnight at a time, they scour the area for sick, injured or starving pandas. Two of the workers were absent on one of these expeditions for the duration of our visit.

Day Nineteen

We are due to start the return journey to Chengdu tomorrow. The flight we had intended to take back to Hong Kong is scheduled to leave in four days. Though we would love to stay longer in the hospital, we have no excuse to do so. We have succeeded beyond our wildest dreams in getting close to the giant pandas, and other native Chinese wildlife. Pollyanna has had an incredible opportunity to study and sketch Yiao. In addition, we have lived in the very heart of the panda's natural territory, waking each morning to look out of our bedroom window at the lush green mountainsides which are home to the wild pandas.

We tell Mr Qing at lunch time that we will be leaving the next day. He immediately announces that a special farewell meal will be prepared for us that evening. The two hospital workers who have been working out on the mountainside are also due to return that night; if they arrive in time they will be able to join us.

永

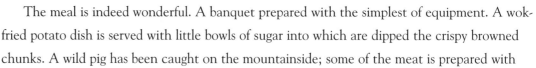

The meal is indeed wonderful. A banquet prepared with the simplest of equipment. A wok-fried potato dish is served with little bowls of sugar into which are dipped the crispy browned chunks. A wild pig has been caught on the mountainside; some of the meat is prepared with green and red peppers. Sichuan's own pork and spring onion dish is served, along with a huge bowl of thin soup, full of tomatoes, wild vegetables picked fresh that morning and vast bowls of rice. More clear alcohol and yak's cheese is boiled up at the end of the meal; this time we have no reservations about accepting a cup. We raise our glasses to one another with the traditional Chinese toast, *gan be*i. Mr Qing makes a special presentation to us of a beautiful carving of a mountain deer raised out of a plaque of wood. He has made it himself. We are very touched, and ask him to sign the back for us. We will treasure it always. He also gives us some photographs of baby Yiao, and we promise to send on some of ours.

More alcohol and yak's cheese is drunk, and the whole party becomes quite maudlin. We are told that we must stay another night. We really can't. We must stay for lunch tomorrow. We will try. We must have a fourth cup of yak's cheese. We had better not. Well we must have a can of peach drink then. We must return to the hospital one day for another visit. We would love to. We must return the following spring. If only we could.

Mr Qing promises that if we do return he will learn English for the occasion so that we can have a proper conversation; he will make another carving for us, in fact he will carve us a marble statue. Even Mr Jing gets into the spirit of the evening and tells us that, although we may never meet again, he will remember the journey with us for the rest of his life. We finally retire to our rooms, overwhelmed by the kindness we have been shown on this remote mountainside.

Unfortunately we do not have another chance to say our goodbyes to Mr Qing the following morning. Our sleep was interrupted by the sound of lorry engines and car horns until 4.00 am – something we had not heard before at the hospital. We learn the following day that Mr Qing received an emergency call at midnight, requesting his help with the initial stages of the transportation of a black bear from Sichuan province to Beijing.

The two workers we had not met during our stay did not get back in time to join in the feast, but returned from their working trip on the mountainside in the early hours of the morning.

MR QING MAKES A SPECIAL PRESENTATION TO US OF A BEAUTIFUL CARVING OF A MOUNTAIN DEER RAISED OUT OF A PLAQUE OF WOOD.

THERE ARE TWO WOODEN BEDS WITH STRAW MATRESSES.

Pollyanna Pickering—.
Fengfengxiou April 19th 1994

Yau Yuan up a Tree.

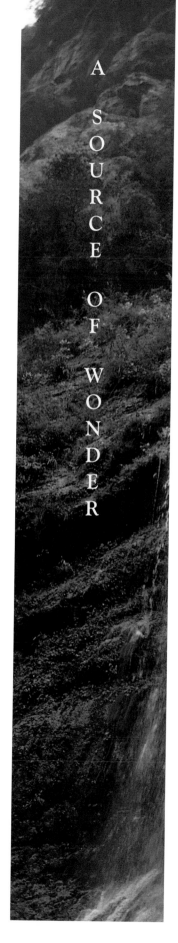

Chapter Fourteen

F 大熊猫

OLLOWING Père David's 'discovery' of the giant panda in 1869, very little additional information about the 'famous white and black bear' came out of China for nearly half a century. Père David returned to France in 1874, due to illness, and was never to recover sufficiently to return to China in order to continue his work. He never succeeded in seeing a live panda.

In 1917, a live cub was presented to a German zoologist by local hunters, but it died in a matter of days. Its skin was sent to the Berlin museum. In 1924, another Christian missionary, J Houston Edgar, wrote to the *China Journal* about a curious animal he had seen while travelling in the Tibetan borderlands in 1916:

...in a wild country not far from the Kin Sha, I saw an animal asleep in the forks of a high oak tree, which has puzzled me ever since. It was very large, seemed quite white, and was curled in a great ball, much in the manner of cats. It was unknown, and a source of wonder to my Tibetans.

If this 'source of wonder' was indeed a giant panda, as has been suggested since, then J Houston Edgar has the honour of being the first Westerner to see a live wild giant panda.

The first confirmed sighting, however, was made jointly in 1929 by two other Americans, Kermit and Theodore Roosevelt, the sons of President Theodore Roosevelt. Unfortunately, their aim in travelling through the largely unexplored borderlands was to gain the so called prestige of being the first big game hunters to bring back a giant panda as a trophy. It took them six months to track down a giant panda, and their quest was ultimately successful.

This 'victory' sparked off a number of hunting expeditions, many of them funded by museums wanting skins or carcasses for their collections. Only a handful of the many hunters who set out met with any degree of success and, thankfully, by the end of the 1930s

永

the enthusiasm for tracking pandas was already fading.

Further expeditions were organised to capture a giant panda and bring it back alive to a Western zoo. After fruitless attempts by several parties of naturalists, Ruth Harkess, the socialite widow of zoologist William Harkess, finally succeeded in tracking down and capturing a panda cub on the 18th December 1936. She cared for the cub herself and brought it home triumphantly to Chicago.

For many decades in the middle of the century, while China struggled in the grip of political turmoil, much of China, including panda country was closed to all foreigners. In more recent years numerous scientists, explorers and naturalists have travelled throughout the remote wilds of China in search of these elusive creatures. They have tried, with varying degrees of success, to capture, study and photograph the panda, or just glimpse them in the bamboo forests. However, since the discovery of the panda in 1869, it is believed that fewer than fifty Western visitors to China have seen one of these elusive animals in the wild.

Day Twenty

We get up early on our last morning at Fentengxiao to say goodbye to the pandas and take a few last photographs, before meeting Daphne and the hospital workers for breakfast. We are joined outside the pens by one of the two men who returned from the mountainside in the early hours of the morning. We greet him as best we can. He points towards the sketch pad Pollyanna is carrying and we show him some of her drawings.

He browses through them, then motions for us to follow him. We walk together past the pens and through the paddock to the large enclosed area where baby Yiao will be living when he is older, prior to his eventual re-release into the wild. We pass out of the enclosure on the far side and cross a wide patch of scrub land, then through a heavy wooden door set into a high concrete wall. As we continue to walk, it slowly dawns on us that we have left the confines of the hospital gates and are moving up into the mountain forests. Although at Wolong we spent a considerable amount of time out on the mountains, during our stay at Fentengxiao we have not ventured outside the hospital, staying within the grounds to work with the baby.

As we follow our new guide the vegetation becomes increasingly dense and difficult to walk

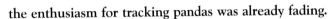

through. The mountainside is dense with bamboo and the tall stems are thick and close growing; they are tangled together in impenetrable thickets and at times our progress is very slow.

There are at least two hundred species of bamboo growing in China, but on these lower mountain slopes it is predominately umbrella bamboo that we are struggling through – one of the two main varieties eaten by the giant panda. Bamboo is a tough evergreen grass which forms the staple diet of the red panda and ninety-eight per cent of all the food eaten by the giant panda. It grows more rapidly than any other living thing – a growth of five centimetres an hour has been recorded. Adult pandas can consume over forty kilos of bamboo in one day and therefore need a copious and constant supply. Because of this the unusual life cycle of bamboo can have a dramatic influence on the survival of the pandas in China.

Unlike most members of the grass family, bamboo plants reproduce most years by sending out underground runners, which then send up new shoots to the surface. However, at intervals bamboo reproduces like other grasses by flowering. The interval between the appearance of the flowers varies from between fifteen and one hundred and twenty years, depending on the individual species, but is always consistent. All the plants of any one species flower at the same time, even in entirely different locations. The following year all the plants die back simultaneously. Even plants exported to other countries have been observed to flower in synchronicity with those remaining in China. The exact trigger causing the plants to flower is still a mystery to scientists, though many different theories have been put forward. Evidently the flowering cannot be triggered by environmental factors as was originally thought; the plants are effectively pre-programmed. These periodic die backs, which have been recorded in Chinese writings for over two thousand years, can cause major problems for the pandas when the flowering cycle of two or more of the species coincides. When this happens they flower, seed and die back at the same time. This last happened in the mid-seventies, with a disastrous effect on the already decreasing panda population.

In earlier times pandas were able to survive mass die backs of bamboo by moving to another area where different species were still growing prolifically. In modern times, however, as farming and industry cuts into more and more of the pandas' habitat, they find themselves trapped in isolated pockets, unable to cross to other feeding grounds. Because they eat such vast quantities

of bamboo they feed almost constantly and cannot cross large areas of land where bamboo is not growing.

The pandas feed mainly on two species of bamboo. Umbrella bamboo grows on the lower slopes of the mountains and flowers approximately every eighty years; arrow bamboo, which grows at higher altitudes, flowers at intervals of approximately forty-five years. Pandas feed for most of the year on the arrow bamboo on the upper slopes of the mountains but in spring will venture down to the lower regions to feed on the new shoots of the umbrella bamboo.

Our self-styled guide leads us steadily upwards; we make our way across clearings and through bamboo thickets. Although at times the vegetation is so dense that the hillside becomes dark, it is turning into a glorious day. The night rains have bowed the bamboo into a dripping green curtain and the air is scented with that particular fresh sweetness that follows a heavy fall of rain. The sun is starting to shine strongly through the morning haze, slanting through the forest canopy and lighting the drops of moisture hanging from the tips of the leaves.

We have been climbing for almost three hours, with no idea of our destination, when suddenly our guide stops. We almost cannon into him as we are absorbed in carefully watching for safe footholds as we walk along the overgrown forest floor. He points upwards through the tangled undergrowth to a taller tree some way ahead of us. At first we are not sure where we are meant to be looking, then Pollyanna clutches my arm. My heart skips a beat. There, in the high branches, I can just make out a pale shape.

Slowly we move towards the tree. I cannot believe my eyes. It seems impossible, when so many people have devoted their lives to searching for wild pandas, that we should be fortunate enough to see one on our very first visit to their homeland.

Hardly breathing, we approach. Gradually the familiar black and white markings take shape and we can clearly make out the curled form of a panda, settled comfortably in the branches.

For most of the year pandas eat and sleep in repeating cycles of eight and four hours through the day and night. Adept at climbing trees, they often nestle in the fork of branches to take their regular rests; here they are safer from roaming predators than they would be sleeping on the ground. The panda's main predators are the Chinese leopard and the dhole, a wild red dog. Both brown and black bears can also pose a threat. However, the panda is far from defenceless. Their

GRADUALLY THE FAMILIAR BLACK AND WHITE MARKINGS TAKE SHAPE . . .

carnivorous origins have left them armed with strong jaws and teeth, and powerful forearms equipped with long and sharp claws. Fortunately it is very rare for an unprovoked panda to attack a human – but people have been killed when they inadvertently placed themselves between a female panda and her cub in a nursery den.

Standing on the mountainside, I feel very aware of our vulnerability. The panda in the tree is clearly a large adult, possibly a male. As we advance slowly and cautiously towards the tree, he watches us as carefully and intently as we watch him. Naturally we are completely unarmed. Even if we had been in possession of a rifle, and the panda had decided to attack, we could not have used it in self-defence without having to face the harsh judgement of Chinese law. In 1987 the supreme court ruled that offenders convicted of killing one panda, or smuggling one skin, would be sentenced to ten or more years in prison. Those convicted of more serious offences would face life imprisonment or even death. As recently as 1989 two farmers convicted of illegally selling panda skins were awarded the death penalty. Luckily, the panda shows no signs of aggression. During the time we stand observing him he moves only once – I draw a sharp intake of breath – but he simply shuffles himself into a more comfortable position and continues to watch us.

We stop not far from the tree. I had been carefully taking photographs as we approached. Now Pollyanna is also able to take out her paper and start to sketch the panda above us in the tree. We remain for just over an hour, standing completely still, gazing in awe at our wild panda. Behind the tree, the mountain range stretches into the distance, the closer inclines appearing darkly forested; the peaks and crags behind paler in the perpetual haze which clings to their slopes even in the clear bright spring sunlight. I knew then that even if none of my photographs was successful this image would remain with me for the rest of my life. Eventually, reluctantly, we turn away and make our way back down the mountain towards the hospital. We see Daphne as we arrive back in the courtyard and race over, talking animatedly about our experience, and brimming over with questions to ask our guide – so far we have communicated only in sign language.

We learn that, on his return to the hospital last night, Mr Qing and the other workers had told him about their two strange blonde guests lodging at the hospital. He had been told all about Pollyanna and her work, about our interest in wildlife and our love of pandas. This morning, he

HARDLY BREATHING WE APPROACH . . .

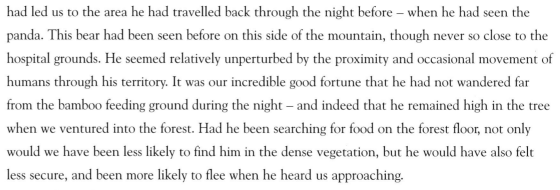

had led us to the area he had travelled back through the night before – when he had seen the panda. This bear had been seen before on this side of the mountain, though never so close to the hospital grounds. He seemed relatively unperturbed by the proximity and occasional movement of humans through his territory. It was our incredible good fortune that he had not wandered far from the bamboo feeding ground during the night – and indeed that he remained high in the tree when we ventured into the forest. Had he been searching for food on the forest floor, not only would we have been less likely to find him in the dense vegetation, but he would have also felt less secure, and been more likely to flee when he heard us approaching.

Finally, we leave Fentengxiao, still trying to convey our grateful thanks to everyone at the hospital. Belatedly we begin the long drive back to Chengdu, from where we will start our long return journey home.

Little more than a week after we stood gazing in awe at the wild giant panda, Pollyanna is sitting once again in her studio, in the heart of the Peak District of Derbyshire. Pinned to her drawing-board are the rough sketches she made standing beneath a tree on a remote mountainside in the Sichuan province. As she prepares to start work the journey through China is already starting to feel like a distant dream. The people, the culture, the spectacular landscapes through which we travelled seem impossibly far away from our home in the English countryside. We are distanced from China by more than a ten-hour flight – a language, a way of life, a system of beliefs all separate us. Yet our travels had succeeded beyond our most optimistic imaginings. We had the good fortune to meet and be welcomed by people committed to protecting and helping Chinese wildlife, who were willing to help us in our search for pandas. Through the eventual success of breeding programmes such as the one initiated at Wolong, and the dedication of people like Mr Qing and his co-workers, we are given hope that the giant panda, loved and recognised by people around the world, will survive in the wild mountains of China for centuries to come.

With these thoughts in her mind, Pollyanna finds the sights, sounds and inspiration of China returning vividly as she picks up her brush to begin work on her first painting of the wild giant panda of Fentengxiao.

THE END

PAINTING THE WILD PANDA OF FENTENGXIAO FROM INITIAL FIELD SKETCHES TO COMPLETION.

Pollyanna Pickering —

'When you are planning to paint
you must always create
a harmonious relationship
between heaven and earth'

GUIO SI
ARTIST OF THE SUNG DYNASTY (970 - 1279)

The wild panda of Fentengxiao

'Even as a mother protects with her life
her child, her only child
So with a boundless heart
Should one cherish all living beings'

FROM THE BUDDHA'S WRITINGS ON METTA (LOVING KINDNESS)
THE SUTTA NIPATA

CHILDREN OF EDEN
IN THE COLLECTION OF THE BRYANS FAMILY (UK)

'Let the states of equilibrium and
harmony exist in perfection and
happy order will prevail through
heaven and earth and all things
will be nourished and flourish'

FROM THE ANALECTS OF CONFUCIOUS
(551 - 479 BC)

BABY LOVE
IN THE COLLECTION OF MRS C MCDONNELL (UK)

'The night rains have bowed the bamboo into a dripping green curtain, and the air is scented with that particular fresh sweetness that follows a heavy fall of rain'

FROM THE DIARY

BAMBOO BEAR
IN THE COLLECTION OF MR & MRS KERSLAKE (UK)

'After all the months of planning, reading, researching and hoping it is incredible to find ourselves face to face with one of these rare creatures in the heart of their homeland'

FROM THE DIARY

BAMBOO

PRIVATE COLLECTION (UK)

'Their beautifully marked rust coloured fur appears to glow red in some lights earning them the colloquial name of Firefox'

FIREFOX
PRIVATE COLLECTION (SOUTH AFRICA)

'The clear moon shines
in the frost
and the frost
reflects the moon
Moon and frost
exchange brightness'

FROM THE COUPLETS OF THE POET T C LAI

FIRST SNOW
PRIVATE COLLECTION (UK)

'To sit carefree in a grove of trees
and attainment of a mind
that is still earns bliss
that is above the heavens'

THE PHILOSOPHER NAGARJUNA
WRITING ON THE MAHAPRAJNAPARAMITA SUTRA

SLEEPYHEAD
PRIVATE COLLECTION (UK)

'Seeing the bamboo groves
where the pandas feed,
and the springs and streams
where they stop and drink
will give Pollyanna a picture
of their lifestyle
and environment which
cannot be gained from
reading books . . .'

FROM THE DIARIES

TREETOPS

IN THE COLLECTION OF MR & MRS BAILEY (UK)

*'The pandas climb with a
cat-like grace and agility
into the top branches
of the trees and settle themselves
into a fork to rest, lying still
while absorbing
the last rays of the
evening sun'*

FROM THE DIARY

SITTING PRETTY

'Try to be mindful and let things take their natural course. Then your mind will become still in any surroundings, like a clear forest pool. All kinds of wonderful rare animals will come to drink at the pool, and you will see clearly the nature of all things

You will see many strange and wonderful things come and go, But you will remain still'

FROM THE WRITINGS OF ACHAAN CHAH
BUDDHIST MEDITATION MASTER, THAILAND

獨賞秋色

茱莉安娜·匹克林

Pollyanna Pickering —.
FenTonoxiou '94

IT'S A WONDERFUL WORLD
PRIVATE COLLECTION (UK)

'The Tao gives birth to all things
nourishes them, maintains them,
Takes them back to itself
Creating without possessing
acting without expecting
Guiding without interfering
That is why the love of the Tao
is in the very nature to things'

Lao Tzu

HEAD OVER HEELS IN LOVE WITH BABY PANDAS
IN THE COLLECTION OF MR & MRS COX (UK)

'I live in the western wilderness
Leopards and tigers are my companions
Crows and magpies my clowns
Briefly you honour me'

A Poem credited to the Goddess XiWangMu,
Traditional Chinese Mythology

NATIONAL TREASURE
IN THE COLLECTION OF MR MARLOW (UK)

'Female pandas are gentle and devoted mothers seemingly aware of the vulnerability of their cubs which they cradle in their giant paws, comforting them with little pats, and frequently licking and nuzzling the tiny babies'

FROM THE DIARY

MOTHER LOVE
IN THE COLLECTION OF MR KIRBY (UK)

'The mind relaxes, the heart delights
All honours and disgrace are forgotten
what pleasure what joy
to sit here and drink in the breeze'

FAN ZHONGYAN (989 - 1052)

ON THE ROCKS
PRIVATE COLLECTION (UK)

'All work at last
is to perfection
brought
Earth fairest prospects
all here are
installed'

FROM THE STORY OF THE STONE
TRADITIONAL CHINESE LEGEND

波莉安娜·匹克琳

別洞觀景

Pollyanna Pickering ——.
Fenfengxiou 1994.

HELP!
PRIVATE COLLECTION (UK)

'The baby panda is in
excellent health
and is full of energy
and curiosity
He rejoices
in the name of
Yiao Yuan ...'

FROM THE DIARIES

PANDA PUZZLE TREE

PRIVATE COLLECTION (UK)

'Small dark eyes peer out inquisitively
from coal black patches
giving the panda a look of wide-eyed
innocence'

FROM THE DIARIES

WINTER IN WOLONG
IN THE COLLECTION OF MISS C M HEWSON (UK)

'From morning glow to evening light
The views change a thousand, ten
thousand times'

FAN ZHONGYAN
(989-1052)

In the Mountains of the Sleeping Dragon
In the collection of Mr & Mrs Bradbury (UK)

'All creatures weak or strong
All creatures great and small
Creatures unseen or seen
Dwelling afar or near
Born or awaiting birth
May you all be blessed with peace'

THE BUDDHA'S TEACHING
SUTTA NIPATA

LITTLE BEAR BEHIND
IN THE COLLECTION OF MR P SHERWELL (UK)

ROUGH AND TUMBLE

In the collection Mr & Mrs Lord (UK)

AFTERWORD

This book is intended to be a personal account of our experiences in China during our quest to find and study giant pandas in their natural habitat. These experiences enabled Pollyanna to create a record in paintings of this remarkable animal which continues to struggle to exist on the edge of extinction.

We were not in China to attempt a scientific study of the panda, or any other animal, and had no direct links with any scientific or zoological organisation.

Where information about the lifestyle and habits of giant pandas has been included I have endeavoured to keep the facts and figures as accurate as possible. However, the panda is one of the world's rarest and least accessible animals. Their numbers are few and they live in isolated pockets in a dense and inhospitable habitat. Whilst researching the facts about the pandas, I soon found that any statistic I found in one book would immediately be contradicted in another, and figures given for life span, breeding habits and diet fluctuated wildly.

Cross-referencing as much as possible, I hope to have avoided any major inaccuracies in the text. I relied a great deal for technical information on the books of George Schaller, director of science at Wildlife Conservation International, a division of the New York Zoological Society, who has probably spent more time studying pandas in the wild than any other Westerner.

His books *The Giant Pandas of Wolong* and *The Last Pandas* are fascinating accounts of both his studies and his fears for the future of the panda.

STUDY OF YIAO YUAN
IN THE COLLECTION OF MR CHARLESWORTH

Baby Pandas very intent on exploring sniffing rocks/plants completely fearless

BIBLIOGRAPHY

Schaller, G B, with Hu Jinchu, Pen Wamshi and Zhu Jing, *The Giant Pandas of Wolong:* University Press of Chicago, 1985

Schaller, G B, *The Last Panda* : University Press of Chicago, 1993

Catton, C, *Pandas:* Christopher Helm Publishing Ltd, 1990

Hu Tieqing (editor), *The Wildlife Treasure House – Reserves in Sichuan:* China Forestry Publishing House, 1991

Tang Xinyang, *Living Treasures:* Bantam Books, 1987

Tang Guang Yiu, Li Wei (editors), *Wildlife of China:* China Forestry Publishing House

Holdsworth, M, *Sichuan:* Odessey, 1993

Jung Chang, *Wild Swans:* Flamingo, 1991

Deh Ta Hsuing, *Chinese Szechwan Cooking:* Paragon, 1994

Radcliffe-Rogers, B, *Giant Pandas:* Mallard Press, 1990

Laidler, K and Laidler, L, *Pandas – Giants of the Bamboo Forest:* BBC Books, 1992

Taylor, D, *The Giant Panda:* Boxtree, 1990

Harkness, R, *The Lady and the Panda:* Nicholson and Watson, 1938

Sheldon, W, *The Wilderness Home of the Giant Panda:* University of Massachusetts Press, 1975

Hewitt, C, *Buddhism:* Wayland, 1995

Gooneewardene, A, *Buddhist Scriptures:* Heineman, 1994

Bancroft, A, *The Buddhist World:* MacDonald, 1984

Plus a wide selection of press/magazine articles including:

Giant Panda: Wildlife Fact File, International Masters Publishing Ltd

Save the Giant Panda: Wildlife Fact File, International Masters Publishing Ltd

Red Panda: Wildlife Fact File, International Masters Publishing Ltd

Wolong Nature Reserve and its Wildlife: Wildlife Fact File, International Masters Publishing Ltd

Wen Huanshu and He Yeheng, *China's Wildlife Yesterday and Today:* China Reconstructs, 1980

Ri Nong, *Saving the Pandas:* China Reconstructs, 1984

Wolong Research Centre: China Reconstructs, January 1994

Xu Weishu, *Protecting Birds and their Habitats:* China Reconstructs, December 1983

Zhang Hemin (editor), *Wolong Panda News:* Volume 1 No 2

Laidler, K, *Giant Pandas Search for a Home:* The Guardian, 28 December 1995

Pandering to their Needs: Wild about Animals, October 1995

Couper-Johnston, R, *Million Dollar Baby:* BBC Wildlife Magazine, November 1995

Reed, T. H, *What's Black and White and Loved All Over?:* National Geographic, November 1972

Pan Wenshi, *China's Last Great Black and White Hope:* Sunday Express, 28 May 1995

Pan Wenshi, *New Hope for China's Giant Pandas*:
National Geographic, February 1995

Schaller, G B, *Secrets of the Wild Panda*: National
Geographic, March 1986

Laidler, K, *Children of The Mountain:* The Guardian,
23 March 1995

Green, J, *Is This the Last Hope?:* Daily Express,
6 January 1996

Kendal, E, *Teddy's Bears:* Observer Magazine,
3 November 1974

ACKNOWLEDGEMENTS

Many people gave us great assistance and support while we were planning our journey and when
travelling through China. Our biggest thanks must go to Yang Ben Qing and all of the workers at
the hospital at Fentengxiao, both for the hospitality and welcome shown to us and their
continuing work to help the panda in the struggle for survival. We could not have made the
journey at all without the hard work of Daphne and Mr Jing, who showed us kindness and
friendship well beyond the call of duty. Thanks are due also to all the staff at Wolong for their
help and interest. The Chinese Embassy was most helpful in providing us with contacts and
advice. Mr Rudi Chan of Cultural Tours was invaluable in organising flights, corresponding with
the local tourism offices, obtaining visas and documentation and finding us such an expert
interpreter. Back home, many people have given their support and encouragement during the
writing of the book, special mention must go to Alyson Gregory for working her way through
pages of original manuscript with such patience and clear vision and to Sue Stainton for her hard
work and exceptional skill in making our book a reality with her original ideas and talent for
layout design. Gary Beck and all at Otter House, our publishers, have shown great faith in the
idea of the book through every stage of the work, from the initial proposals through to
publication. To Rosemary Lee our thanks for her patience and dedication. Additional thanks to
Bill Jordan for his helpful information about the release of Père David's deer into China, and all
at Care for the Wild for their continuing work with animals in Britain and around the world.

当心你吃的猪肉

狗年宠物